simply
stitched
gifts

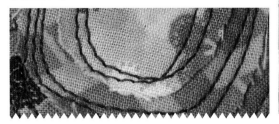

simply
stitched
gifts

21 Fun Projects Using Free-Motion Stitching

CYNTHIA SHAFFER

LARK
New York

LARK
New York

An Imprint of Sterling Publishing
1166 Avenue of the Americas
New York, NY 10036

Text and photography © 2015 by Cynthia Shaffer
Illustrations © 2015 by Sterling Publishing

Book design by Karla Baker

ISBN 978-1-4547-0904-6

Distributed in Canada by Sterling Publishing
c/o Canadian Manda Group, 664 Annette Street
Toronto, Ontario, Canada M6S 2C8
Distributed in the United Kingdom by
GMC Distribution Services Castle Place,
166 High Street, Lewes, East Sussex, England BN7 1XU
Distributed in Australia by Capricorn Link (Australia) Pty. Ltd.
P.O. Box 704, Windsor, NSW 2756, Australia

For information about custom editions, special sales, and premium and corporate
purchases, please contact Sterling Special Sales at 800-805-5489
or specialsales@sterlingpublishing.com.

Manufactured in China

2 4 6 8 10 9 7 5 3 1

larkcrafts.com

contents

introduction

— —— —— —— — —— —— —— —— —— —— —— —— ——

Of all the gifts we give and receive, handmade stitched gifts rank pretty high on my list, and gift giving is the perfect excuse to stitch!

— —— —— —— — —— —— —— —— —— —— —— —— ——

Whenever I sit down at my sewing machine, I get a bit nostalgic and start thinking of my childhood. I'm reminded just how much I love to sew. I've always loved to make things—from clothing for my dolls as a child, to quilts and pillows for my home. But one of my favorite things to do is make something special for a loved one. When I was in high school, I decided to sew a shirt for my father for Christmas. I didn't have much money, and a handmade shirt seemed like the perfect compromise. I cut the pattern out on my bedroom floor and sewed that shirt while he was at work. My father loved that shirt so much, and every time he wore it, he proudly let everyone know his daughter made it for him.

Stitched Gifts mixes my two loves of stitching and sewing with free-motion stitching. I know, I know—free-motion stitching can be a bit intimidating, but I'm here to help you get over your stress and anxiety. The Basics section (page 8) will help guide you through your first free-motion stitching experience. And if you're a pro at free-motion stitching, then play along and get creative with my ideas and images, or use your own sketches to really personalize your stitched gifts.

Your gifts will be unique and original thanks to the liberating feeling of free-motion stitching.

Personalize your gifts with a likeness of a friend's pet that is appliquéd to an irresistible pillow (page 110).

Adorable felt owl-and-feather bookmarks are the perfect accessories for all the sweet gals in your Friday night book club (page 34).

Stitch a special cloud-and zoo-themed flannel and terry-cloth set for that friend that's ready to pop out a little one (page 45).

A set of quick, colorful, stitched modern greeting cards is perfect for that hard-to-buy-for friend in your gift exchange (page 96).

Whip up a modern "mug rug" to welcome the new office mate; wrap it around an oversize mug filled with some homemade biscotti (page 98).

So flip through the pages and get inspired by all the gifts you can stitch in little to no time!

— —— —— —— — —— —— —— —— —— —— —— —— ——

basics

In the following sections you will find some basic information required to create your own stitched gifts. You will need a few essential tools to tackle the sewing portion of all the projects in this book. Most sewers have these items lying around, but there are a few projects that require specific tools, which are listed at the beginning of the projects under the heading What You Need.

Just beyond the basic sewing information you will find everything you need to know about free-motion stitching.

note: *If you do not want to learn free-motion stitching right now, but you love to stitch gifts, consider hand- or machine-embroidering the motifs. Or, if you wish to just make the gifts without any stitchy goodness, simply use a fabric with a fun print on it instead. For example, the image on the Pet Portrait Pillow (page 110) could easily be stitched to the pillow front using embroidery floss and a blanket stitch. Same goes for the Road Trippin' Hoop Art on page 116. The Cloud & Elephant Bib & Burp Cloth set (page 44) would look sweet with little hand-stitched or machine-embroidered elephants in place of free-motion-styled ones.*

But for now, here's a list of sewing items that will help you get started with your stitched gifts and allow your personality to shine through them.

basic sewing kit

Sewing machine (NOT PICTURED) • Scissors (1) • Free-motion pressure foot or darning foot (not pictured)

Straight pins (2) • Rotary cutter (3) • Self-healing cutting mat (4) • See-through quilters' ruler (5)

Measuring tape (6) • Hand-sewing needles (7) • Iron and ironing board (not pictured)

Sharp pencil (8) • White paper (9)

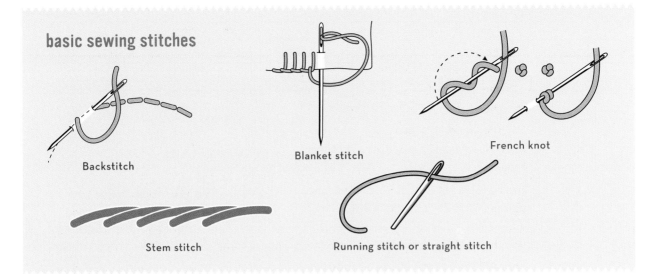

basic sewing stitches

Backstitch

Blanket stitch

French knot

Stem stitch

Running stitch or straight stitch

Basic Sewing Information

Because this is a book of stitched gifts and free-motion stitching, I need to give you a bit of general sewing information.

- If a particular seam allowance is required, it is noted at the beginning of the project.

- When a seam is being sewn with a normal straight stitch, use your favorite straight-stitch presser foot and an average stitch length, which corresponds to a number 3 on your sewing machine stitch-length dial.

- There are a few projects that will tell you to baste the fabric, in which case you will lengthen the stitch, which corresponds to a number 4 or 5 on your sewing machine stitch-length dial.

- Top stitching is mentioned in a few of the instructions. This simply means that you stitch the projects with the right side up and with an average stitch length, which corresponds to a number 3 on your sewing machine stitch-length dial.

Essential Free-Motion Stitching Information

The free-motion stitching element of the projects in this book is where the real fun comes in. I know so many sewers want to jump on the free-motion train but feel intimidated, or they just don't know where to start. Well, this book is just the place to start!

Let me chat a bit about my understanding of the difference between free-motion stitching, free-motion machine embroidery, and free-motion quilting. The term *free motion* simply means that you—the sewer, not the feed dogs on the sewing machine—are moving the fabric or paper around while the sewing machine is stitching. The feed dogs are disengaged, therefore allowing *you* to control the movement of the fabric!

- Free-motion stitching is simply stitching freely on layers of fabric or paper.

- To me, free-motion machine embroidery encompasses free-motion stitching on fabric but also filling in the area that you're stitching by moving the fabric back and forth several times, creating a solid embroidered look.

- And finally, free-motion quilting is much the same as free-motion stitching except that there is a layer of batting under the top piece. Free-motion quilting is often done on large sewing machines, like long-arm quilting machines, and usually follows a traced stitch pattern.

Binding Information

A few projects in this book will need binding around the outer edge. After you have cut the binding strip according to the project directions, come back to this section and finish up the binding process as explained below.

1   Cut one end at a diagonal and then press the end under ¼ inch (6 mm). Press the binding in widthwise.

2   Pin the folded binding to one of the long edges; start the binding at the diagonally cut end. Align the cut edge of the binding with the outer edge. Place one pin at the corner of the binding and the project, ¼ inch (6 mm) from the corner.

3   Begin stitching the binding in place. Start 2 inches (5.1 cm) away from the diagonally cut edge, continue until you reach the end pin, and then back-tack a few stitches. Take the pin out.

4   Lift the presser foot up, pull the thread out a few inches, and turn the project.

5   Lift the binding straight up and off the project, and then fold it straight down, aligning the cut edge of the binding with the outer edge of the project.

6   Continue stitching for a few inches and then stop, but leave the needle in the project, pin the binding to the edge, and place a pin ¼ inch (6 mm) from the corner. Continue stitching until you reach the end pin and then back-tack a few stitches. Take the pin out.

7   Repeat steps 4–6 two more times.

8   After the last corner is turned, continue stitching the binding in place until you reach the diagonal, pressed edge. Lay the remaining binding onto the project to estimate where the binding needs to be cut. Make sure that the binding overlaps the diagonal cut completely. Slip the binding into the diagonal binding and then continue to sew through all the layers.

9   Trim the corners at a diagonal.

10 Fold the binding over the edge of the project and pin in place on the back side.

11 Fold the binding in at the corners to create mitered corners.

12 Hand sew the binding in place.

Tools, Techniques, and Materials

Sewing Machine Needles

There are a variety of sewing machine needles out there to choose from. Some free-motion quilters prefer to use standard sharp needles, some prefer topstitch needles, and others, like me, prefer to use a universal needle in a 90/14 size. This needle is a good general sewing machine needle and can accommodate a variety of threads. It also has a sturdy shaft so it can hold up well while stitching through layers of fabric, as well as paper and card stock.

Free-Motion Presser Foot

The presser foot needed to free-motion stitch has a variety of names, and while they might look a bit different, they all essentially serve the same purpose. Depending on the sewing machine manufacturer, some call this a darning foot or a free-motion quilting foot. There is even a free-motion foot called a Big Foot. Some of these presser feet have a crescent shape to them, which allows you to see where you are stitching, and some of them have a small metal or plastic circle that the needle passes through. If your machine did not come with a free-motion foot, they are readily available on the Internet; just make sure that the part number matches up with your particular sewing machine.

Feed Dogs

I love the name of this little sewing machine part! The feed dogs are the little strip of metal teeth that rise up from the throat plate to grip the fabric and move it along while sewing; machines typically use a set of these. While most sewing is done with the feed dogs in the raised position, free-motion stitching is done with the feed dogs down, or covered up. When the feed dogs are down, the sewer is in full control of the stitching and movement of the fabric or paper.

Templates

Many of the projects in this book require some sort of template to be made. Templates for the projects can be found beginning on page 132. Enlargement percentages are listed near the template in order to make the project exactly the same size as the sample I made. You may want to make your piece even larger or smaller.

The easiest way to create a template is to trace the template onto copy paper and then cut out the paper template. Depending on the color of your fabric, you can then either trace around the template with a water-soluble fabric marker or, if the fabric is a dark color, trace around the template with a white chalk fabric pencil. Then cut out the fabric on the line of the traced shape.

Another method is to simply pin the traced template to the fabric and then cut around the shape.

Image Transferring

There are various ways to transfer images and motifs to fabric. I think just about every project in this book requires one—or even a couple—of these methods. Depending on the type and color of fabric, some methods will work better than others.

A

B

C

WINDOW OR LIGHT BOX

Trace the motif or image onto a piece of paper and then tape the paper to a well-lit window or a light box. FIG. A Place your fabric on top of the image and, using a water-soluble fabric marker, trace around the image. When you are finished with the free-motion stitching, you can simply dab the stitching with a damp cloth and the marker will disappear.

WAX-FREE CARBON PAPER

This method is ideal when working with fine line-drawn images and dark fabric. Non-wax carbon paper comes in white, yellow, and navy blue, so it will work for both dark and light fabrics. Once you have traced the image or motif onto a piece of paper, place the fabric on a smooth, sturdy, flat surface, right side up, then place the carbon paper on top of the fabric, carbon side down, and finally comes the traced motif or image. Using a ball-point pen, trace over the original traced line, pushing hard to transfer the image to the fabric. FIG. B Once the motif is stitched, you can dab the stitching with a damp cloth and the carbon will disappear.

LIGHTWEIGHT WATER-SOLUBLE STABILIZER SUCH AS SULKY SOLVY

I know, I know . . . this should be in the fabric stiffener section (page 14), but truth be told, this particular product is not very stiff at all! In fact it feels like plastic bag material. But it works great to transfer a motif or image that needs to be free-motion stitched, as in the Beach Cruiser Pouch (page 126). Cut out a piece of water-soluble stabilizer slightly larger than the motif or image. Using a permanent marker, trace the motif or image onto the stabilizer. Pin and stitch the stabilizer to the right side of the fabric around the perimeter using a long basting stitch (FIG. C) and then free-motion stitch the motif or image. Once you are done stitching, rinse the fabric in warm water, and the stabilizer dissolves like magic.

Thread Tension

Yes, the rumors are true: maintaining consistent thread tension while free-motion stitching can be a bit frustrating. And I will say that since we are often only stitching on fabric, without batting sandwiched between fabrics, balancing the tension can be challenging. But remember that there are not any free-motion police out there, so do your best to achieve a balanced stitch and then dive into the projects.

More often than not, the tension on the top thread needs to loosen. If you are using the same thread on the top as in the bobbin, as I recommend, then make some stitched samples to help you get the right tension. Practice free-motion stitching on a piece of felt. Look at the stitches and see if the tension is balanced; in other words, see if the bobbin thread is showing on the top of the felt or if the top thread is being pulled to the underside of the felt. If you see that the top thread is just a straight line of thread and the bobbin thread is coming up through the needle holes, this means that the top-thread tension is too tight. Loosen the top tension, stitch another sample, and check the stitches again. Continue until the stitches are balanced. If the bobbin thread appears to be a straight line, tighten up the top thread. Once a balanced stitch is achieved, make a note of the tension number so that, in the future, you can easily set the dial for the perfect tension.

Now, having said all that, you'll see on a few projects that I actually want the bobbin thread to poke up out of the needle holes; see, for example, the stitching on the Floral-Painted Tablet Cover (page 72). If you look closely, you will see gray thread (from the bobbin) poking up through the holes. I liked the look—the fuchsia thread is muted a bit by the gray dots. And since the cover will not be washed (because of the painted flowers), I don't have to worry that the stitching is going to come loose or pull out.

Gloves

I'm not really a gadget kind of girl; I like to keep my tools to a minimum, but there's one tool I can't live without—my free-motion quilting gloves or sewing gloves. FIG. D
So this is how it goes: I want to free-motion stitch something, you know, like really quick. So I sit down at my sewing machine, drop my dogs, pop on the free-motion presser foot, and just start. Halfway through stitching, I start licking my hands, trying to get a better grip on the fabric! I know—gross, but it's the truth, and I know I'm not alone here! So I look up at the corkboard next to my machine, grab my gloves, and then I'm back in business, wondering why I didn't just start the project wearing the gloves in the first place! Well, maybe now that I have written it down, it will sink in that I need to wear my gloves from the start!

There are a few different types of quilting gloves out there that basically do the same thing. They all have a rubber-like coating at the finger that allows you to grip the fabric without actually pinching or grabbing the fabric. The gloves give you "sticky fingers" to move the fabric up, back, and side to side easily.

Fabric Stiffeners

Because I am often working on a single layer of fabric, I stiffen the fabric before I free-motion stitch to prevent the fabric from buckling and puckering. Here's what I suggest for that purpose:

SPRAY STARCH

I have spray starch handy all the time. A quick spray to the top of the fabric will add body to your fabric and prevent big puckers.

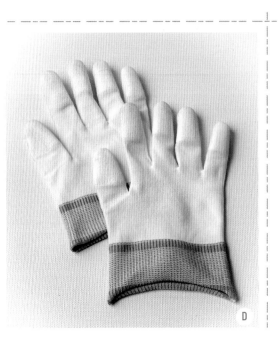

LIGHTWEIGHT FUSIBLE INTERFACING

There are a couple projects that call for lightweight interfacing to give just a little body to the fabric before free-motion stitching. This interfacing is permanent and cannot be removed after stitching.

TEAR-AWAY STABILIZER

There are a few different types of tear-away stiffeners on the market. Tear-away needs to be stitched to the back side of the fabric; after the free-motion stitching is finished, you just pull and tear away the stiffener. Depending on how intricate the free-motion stitching is, it can be a bit of work to tear this backing away completely.

Fabric Adhesives

Many of the projects in this book have raw-edge appliquéd shapes and motifs that require an adhesive to keep the appliqué in place until the free-motion stitching is complete. Here are some products I use:

FUSIBLE WEB

When you want the raw-edge appliqué to really stick to the fabric and to withstand multiple machine washings, then this is the adhesive to use. Flip the image over so the wrong side is up and trace your shapes onto the paper side of the web. Follow the manufacturer's directions and then fuse, or iron, the web side to the wrong side of the fabric. Once the fabric cools, cut around the shape, peel off the paper backing, and then iron the piece to your fabric.

FABRIC GLUE STICK

Truth be told, sometimes I am moving so fast that I just grab any glue stick near me to tack the fabric in place! I think because most of the projects in this book are not wearable, a regular glue stick works perfectly fine. The glue stick is simply needed to attach a bit of fabric just long enough to get the fabric under the sewing-machine presser foot.

TEMPORARY OR PERMANENT SPRAY ADHESIVES

If you are working on a large piece, like the Fabric Collage Bulletin Board (page 38), then spray adhesive is your friend. Make sure you are working in a well-ventilated area and protect the work surface; the spray travels and gets nearby things sticky.

Thread

As I'm sure you're aware, there are so many thread choices in the world now that it can be overwhelming to pick just the right one for free-motion stitching. FIG. E Thankfully, there aren't any free-motion police out there, so don't feel too intimidated. But a good place to start is with a quality cotton thread like Aurifil. There are different weights of thread, as well, but stick with one weight—like 40 or 50—and you'll cover most of your needs.

There is a lot of talk about using a lightweight thread in the bobbin, but I find that if I use the same thread on the sewing machine as in the bobbin, I get the best results. Also, if you stick with one thread type, then once tension adjustments are made, you can easily dial in these adjustments and be ready to free-motion stitch. If your tension is off just a bit and the bobbin thread matches the top thread, then no one will be able to see the bobbin thread poking up through the needle holes.

Fabrics

I've discovered that just about any fabric can be free-motion stitched. FIG. F So, depending on the project you're making, you may need quilting cotton, burlap, muslin, wool suiting,

canvas, felt, velvet, osnaburg, linen, or even store-bought cloth napkins. Some projects use a couple of fabrics together, so have fun with combining textures and different fabric weights.

Paper and Transparencies

Yes, I love to stitch on paper and transparencies. While paper is just fine to practice on, heavier paper, like card stock or even watercolor paper, is a bit more stable for free-motion stitching. Transparencies can be stitched on as well, but I need to warn you that there is a little popping noise that happens when you are stitching. The free-motion foot does tend to jump up and down more than it does when stitching on card stock.

Acrylic Paint

As you look through the book, you'll notice that a few projects have some painting going on as well. Remember, I am not a purist when it comes to free-motion stitching, and the same can be said about my paints. Craft-quality acrylic paint is what I use for most painted projects; I am usually more concerned with finding the right color than the quality of the paint. You will also notice that the projects that include paint are projects that will never need to be washed.

Practice Free-Motion Stitching

Probably the best piece of advice I can give you about free-motion stitching is to practice—practice even for just ten minutes here and there, every day.

For first timers, copy the practice sheet (page 18) onto regular photo paper. With a standard pencil, trace over the lines without lifting the pencil; try to find a path to link the shapes together without lifting the pencil. If you want to create your own free-motion

G

patterns, sketch them first onto paper, drawing them without lifting the pencil.

Okay, now lower the feed dogs and attach the free-motion presser foot. Take the bobbin out of the machine and remove the top thread. Begin free-motion stitching with no thread, following the copied lines on the practice sheet and thinking about the paths you drew in the exercise above.

At first this will feel very awkward and jerky, but as you become more comfortable, increase the speed and move the paper around a little faster.

• Keep as relaxed as possible and remember to breathe.

• As you increase the speed of the sewing machine, you need to increase the movement of the paper.

• If it feels as if you are sketching with your non-dominant hand, then you are doing it right! This is what I love about free-motion stitching.

• Make another copy of the practice sheet and start all over again!

Next, Practice Free-Motion Stitching on Fabric with Thread!

Before I start free-motion stitching on a project, I do a few warm-ups on felt. Here are my tips and tricks to help you out a bit.

Have a stack of pre-cut 6 x 6-inch (15.2 x 15.2-cm) felt squares near the sewing machine at all times. Felt is the best material to practice on because it has a bit of grip and yet it slides around on the sewing machine surface with ease. FIG. G

Fill the bobbin with the same thread that will be used for the sewing machine needle. Thread the sewing machine and draw the bobbin thread up through the hole in the throat plate.

- Put on your sewing gloves!
- Begin free-motion stitching with your hands on the felt, one on either side of the presser foot.
- Relax and go slow at first. Move the felt around slowly while pushing down on the pedal.
- Push down on the felt as you are stitching to get a little resistance from the sewing machine surface.
- Try to match the speed of the pedal to the speed of your hands.
- Increase the speed of the sewing machine and increase the movement of the felt square.
- Stitch in circles, loops, and zigzags; try to spell a word.

If you make the sewing machine go fast and yet you move the felt slowly, the stitches will be close together. The closer together the stitches are, the smaller the motif you can free-motion stitch.

Think of it this way: the felt is the sketch pad and the sewing machine needle is the writing utensil.

Free-Motion Stitching Stitched Gifts

Now that you have practiced free-motion stitching on felt, you are ready to move onto a project in the book. Here are just a few tips and tricks to remember.

When you start free-motion stitching, take three or four stitches in one place to secure the thread. Trim the top thread tail close to the fabric.

Free-motion stitch around the traced image or the raw-edge appliqué. Double-back and stitch again on top of the first stitching to create a sketchy look. Remember, this is not a perfect embroidered look, and the sketchier it is, the more character your piece will have.

When you are finished stitching, take three or four stitches in one place to secure the thread.

Flip the pieces over and clip the threads on the back.

Check out the stitching on the back of the fabric. Countless times I fall in love with the look of the stitching on the back side! FIG. H

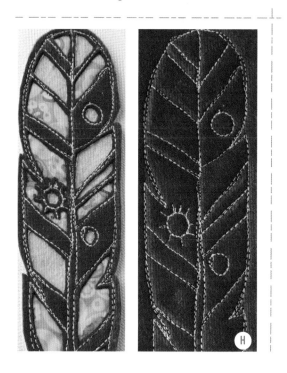

projects

ant table runner

Dress-up any table with a fun runner.
The ants add a playful element!

what you need

Basic Sewing Kit (page 9)

Ant Table Runner templates A-G (page 132)

⅛ yard (11.4 cm) each of 8 coordinating fabrics in orange, gray, tan, brown, and yellow

White cotton fabric, 36½ x 14½ inches (92.7 x 36.8 cm)

Tan print cotton fabric for the backing, 37½ x 15½ inches (95.3 x 39.4 cm)

Scraps of fabrics in dark gray, dark brown, gold, bright orange print, and green print for the ant bodies

¼ yard (22.9 cm) of gray print fabric for the binding

Cotton batting, 37½ x 15½ inches (95.3 x 39.4 cm)

Thread in tan and black

Fabric glue stick

Water-soluble marker

Safety pins

Damp cloth

what you do

note: *Use a ¼-inch (6-mm) seam allowance.*

1 Using the rotary cutter and self-healing cutting mat, cut out sixteen rectangles that measure 2½ x 4½ inches (6.4 x 11.4 cm) and eight squares that measure 2½ x 2½ inches (6.4 x 6.4 cm) from the coordinating fabrics.

2 With right sides facing and short ends aligned, stitch together two rectangles. Stitch another rectangle to the other short end of the piece on the right. Now stitch a square to this piece on the right. Press the seam allowances to one side. Set the strip aside. This is the start of the pieced right side of the runner. FIG. 1

3 With right sides facing and short ends aligned, stitch together one square and one rectangle. Press the seam allowance to one side.

4 Pin this strip to the strip that was sewn together in step 2, right sides together, placing the square from the strip made in step 3 on top of the left-most rectangle. Back-tacking at the beginning and the end of the seam, stitch the strips together, starting ¼ inch (6 mm) from the end of the top rectangle. Stitch all the way to the very end of the top square. Press the seam allowance open.

5 With right sides facing, pin a rectangle on top of this piece, over the left-most square. Stitch the pieces together, starting ¼ inch (6 mm) from the end of top rectangle. Back-tacking at the beginning and the end of the seam, stitch all the way to the very end of the rectangle. Press the seam allowance open. FIG. 2

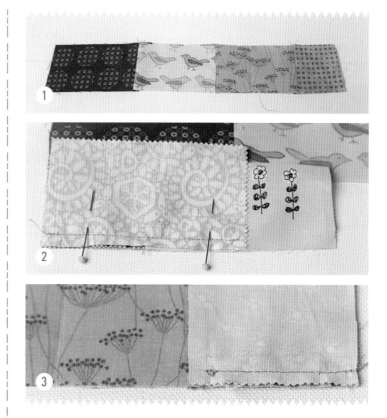

6 With right sides facing, pin a rectangle to this piece. Align the short end of the rectangle on top of the piece created in step 5. Back-tacking at the beginning and the end of the seam, sew the strips together, starting ¼ inch (6 mm) from the end. Press the seam allowance open.

7 On the opposite end, with right sides facing, pin a square on top of the piece. Back-tacking at the beginning and the end of the seam, sew the strips together, starting at the very end but stopping ¼ inch (6 mm) from the end at the opposite end of the square. Back-tack at the beginning and the end of the seam. Press the seam allowance open. FIGS. 3 & 4

8 Flip the pieced section over, wrong side up. Press all the raw edges in by ¼ inch (6 mm). Do not press the outer edge under. Set this piece aside. FIG. 5

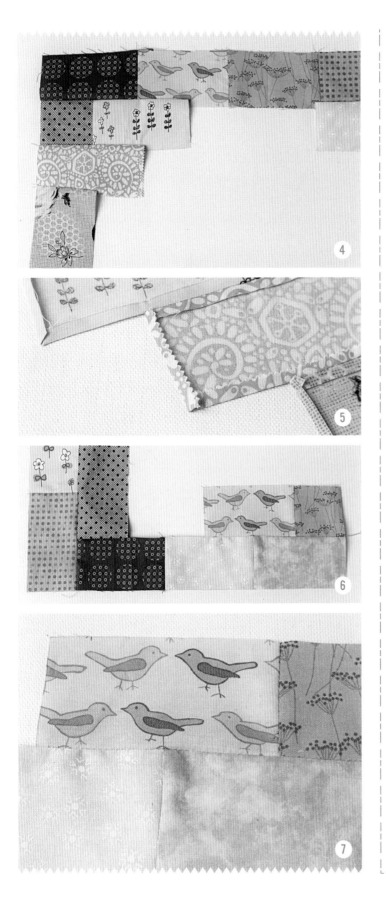

9   With right sides facing, pin a square to a rectangle piece, aligning the short sides. Stitch the pieces together. Stitch a square to the opposite end of this rectangle. Press the seam allowances to one side. Press the top and bottom and left side raw edges under ¼ inch (6 mm).

10   With right sides facing, stitch three rectangles in a row, short ends together. Press the seam allowances to one side. Flip the piece right side up. This is the start of the pieced left side of the runner.

11   With right sides facing, place a rectangle on top of the left-side piece, aligning the short end of the rectangle to the long edge of the stitched rectangle. Make sure that the left sides are aligned. Back-tacking at the beginning, stitch the strips together; stop stitching ¼ inch (6 mm) from the end and back-tack at the end. Press the seam allowances open.

12   With right sides facing, stitch together two squares. Aligning the short ends, stitch a rectangle to this piece and then stitch another rectangle to this rectangle. Press the seam allowances to one side. Flip this piece right side up.

13   Place the piece that was stitched in step 11 on top of the strip from step 12, aligning the pieces at the bottom left corner. Start stitching ¼ inch (6 mm) in from the end of the top rectangle, continue stitching to the very end, and back-tack at the beginning and at the end. Press the seam allowances open.

14   With right sides facing, stitch together one rectangle and one square. Press the seam allowances to one side.

15 With right sides facing, place the strip from step 14 on top of the piece made in step 13 at the right-hand side. Back-tacking at the beginning and at the end, start stitching ¼ inch (6 mm) from the beginning. Press the seam allowances open. FIGS. 6 & 7

16 Flip the pieced section over, wrong side up. Press all the raw edges in by ¼ inch (6 mm). Do not press the outer edge under. Set this piece aside.

17 There are 2 rectangles remaining. For one rectangle, press the raw edges in ¼ inch (6 mm) along both short ends and one long end. For the second rectangle press the raw edges in ¼ inch (6 mm) along both long edges and one short edge.

18 Pin the stitched piece from step 8 to the far right end of the white cotton runner panel. **note:** *There will be ¼ inch (6 mm) of white fabric poking out around the outer edge of the stitched piece.*

19 Pin the stitched piece from step 16 to the far left end of the white cotton runner panel. **note:** *There will be ¼ inch (6 mm) of the white fabric poking out around the outer edge of the stitched piece.* FIG. 8

20 Pin the long stitched strip from step 9 to the bottom of the white cotton runner panel, 3¼ inches (8.3 cm) from the pinned piece at the left end.

21 To the bottom of the white runner panel, pin the rectangle that has the two short ends pressed in from step 17 6½ inches (16.5 cm) from the strip piece at the far right side. Pin the strip ¼ inch (6 mm) from the raw edge of the white cotton runner.

22 Pin the remaining rectangle from step 17 to the top of the white cotton runner 4¾ inches (12 cm) from the

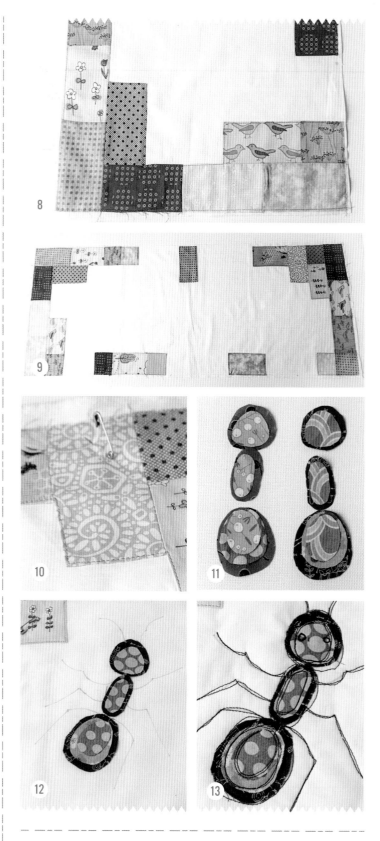

stitched piece on the left. Pin the strip ¼ inch (6 mm) from the raw edge of the white cotton runner.

23 With tan thread on the sewing machine and in the bobbin, stitch the pinned pieces in place, ⅛ inch (3 mm) from the folded edges, pivoting at the corners.

24 With a basting stitch, sew around the perimeter of the piece, ¼ inch (6 mm) from the edge of the white piece. FIG. 9

25 Place the backing fabric on a flat surface, wrong side up. Place the batting on top of the backing fabric. Now center the top piece on top of the batting. Pin the layers together with safety pins. FIG. 10

26 From the various darker fabrics cut out templates A–G for one ant. **note:** *Templates A, D, and F are all cut from the same fabric; templates C, E, and G are cut from the same fabric; template B is cut from a separate fabric, if desired.*

27 Using a glue stick, adhere the ant parts to the top of the table runner as shown in the photograph. Apply glue to each layer to make sure that it stays together while stitching. FIG. 11

28 Refer to the illustration and, using a water-soluble fabric marker, draw in the antennae and the three sets of legs. FIG. 12

29 With black thread on the sewing machine and in the bobbin, free-motion stitch around the ant. Start by stitching around the inner body parts, then work your way to the outer layers. Stitch around each piece several times to create a sketchy look. Free-motion stitch the antennae, legs, and eyes. FIG. 13

30 Repeat steps 26–29 for the remaining three ants. Trim the threads close to the stitching.

31 Flip the runner over to the back side and check out how cute the ants look!

32 Dab the water-soluble marks with a damp cloth and lightly press the runner.

33 With tan thread on the sewing machine and in the bobbin, free-motion stitch a trail of small flowers and leaves 1½ inches (3.8 cm) from the outer edge all the way around the runner and onto the stitched pieces. Stitch a small flower at each corner. FIG. 14

34 Sew a basting stitch around the perimeter of the table runner, through all layers.

35 From the gray binding fabric, cut a strip that measures 2¼ inches wide x 3½ yards (5.7 cm x 3.2 m) long. **note:** *You will have to cut several shorter strips and then stitch them together to make a strip that measures 3½ yards (3.2 m) long.*

36 Bind the outer edge, following the instructions in the Basics section (page 11). Lightly press the table runner. FIG. 15

french press apron

A French press is as classic as an apron.
Give a hostess something fashionable to wear!

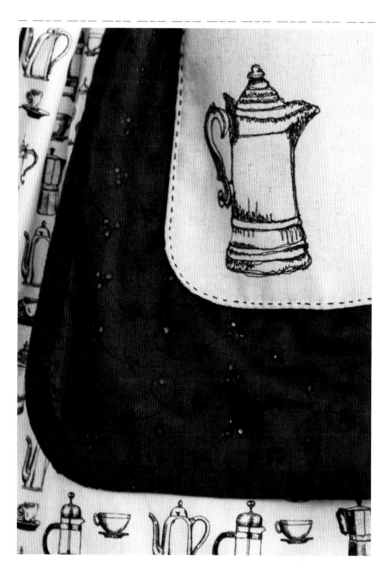

what you need

Basic Sewing Kit (page 9)

French Press Template (page 133)

⅓ yard (30.5 cm) of tan
linen fabric

1 yard (91.4 cm) of black
eyelet fabric

1¼ yards (1.1 m) French-press
print fabric

⅓ yard (30.5 cm) of lightweight
fusible interfacing

Thread in black and tan

Black perle cotton

2 yards (1.8 m) of black
single-fold bias tape

2 yards (1.8 m) of cream
single-fold bias tape

2 yards (1.8 m) of black
soutache braid

Water-soluble fabric marker

White chalk fabric pencil

Coffee cup

Embroidery needle

what you do

1 From the tan linen fabric cut one panel for the pocket that measures 6½ x 8 inches (16.5 x 20.3 cm). Cut one panel from the lightweight interfacing that measures 6½ x 8 inches (16.5 x 20.3 cm).

2 Trace the French press template onto a sheet of paper.

3 Following the manufacturer's directions, fuse the interfacing to the wrong side of the pocket piece.

4 Transfer the French press motif to the pocket from step 1, using the light-box technique (page 13). Mark the motif with a water-soluble fabric marker, 1 inch (2.5 cm) up from the bottom cut edge and 1¼ inch (3.2 cm) from the left side. FIG. 1

5 With black thread on the sewing machine and in the bobbin, free-motion stitch the French press motif. Refer to the close-up photo to fill in the shadows and details in the press. Trim the threads close to the stitching. FIG. 2

6 Place the coffee cup at the bottom right corner and trace the curve of the cup with the water-soluble marker. Repeat for the bottom left corner, then cut off the traced curves. FIGS. 3 & 4

7 Fold the top edge under ¼ inch (6 mm) and press in place. Now fold this top edge back onto the pocket, right sides facing, 1 inch (2.5 cm) down. Pin in place at the sides. FIG. 5

8 With tan thread on the sewing machine and in the bobbin, stitch the side seam with a ¼-inch (6-mm) seam allowance. Continue stitching down the side, around the curve, across the bottom, and then up the opposite side.

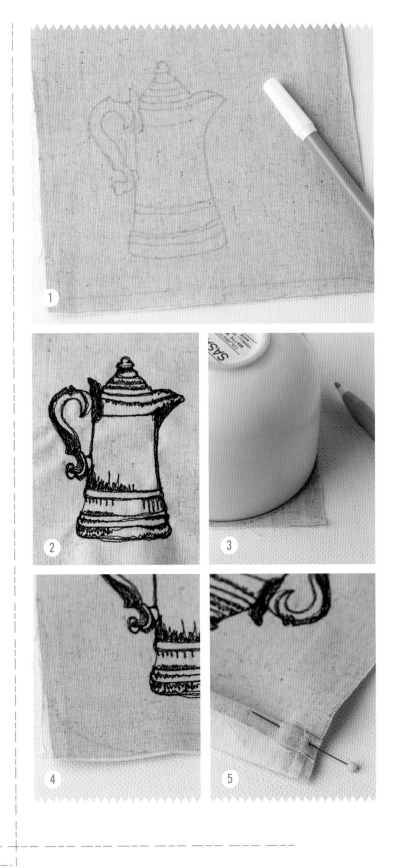

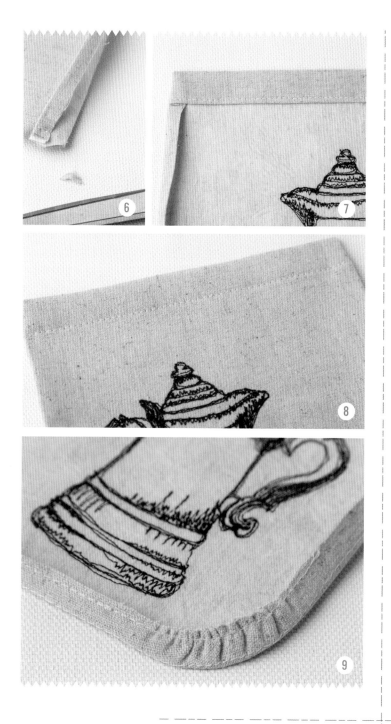

9 Clip the corners diagonally and then flip the top hem right side out. Use a straight pin to poke the corners out. FIG. 6

10 Stitch down the top edge ¾ inch (1.9 cm) from the fold. FIGS. 7 & 8

11 Stitch the pocket again at the two lower corners close to the cut edge, using a basting stitch. Gently pull on the top thread and gather up the stitching; this will allow the curve of the pocket to be nice and rounded. Press the pocket edges in along the inner stitch line. FIG. 9

12 Using the black perle cotton and embroidery needle, stitch a long running stitch (page 10) over the top hem stitching.

13 From the black eyelet fabric, cut a panel that measures 20 x 15 inches (50.8 x 38.1 cm). This piece will be the outer apron.

14 Place the coffee cup at the corners and mark the curve of the cup with the chalk fabric pencil. Cut along the curves.

15 Unfold one side of the black bias tape and pin it, with right sides facing, to the outer edge of the black eyelet panel. With black thread on the sewing machine and in the bobbin, stitch the bias tape in place along the bias fold.

16 Along the outer edge of the bias tape, stitch a basting stitch at both curves. Pull on the top thread to cinch in the bias tape to allow it to lay flat.

17 Fold the bias tape to the wrong side of the panel and then stitch it in place close to the bias tape folded edge.

18 Pin the pocket to the front of the black eyelet panel, 3 inches (7.6 cm) in from the left side and 4 inches (10.2 cm) up from the bottom. FIG. 10

19 With tan thread on the sewing machine and in the bobbin, stitch the pocket in place, ⅛ inch (3 mm) from the outer edge.

20 Using the black perle cotton and embroidery needle, stitch a long running stitch around the pocket on top of the tan stitching. FIG. 11

21 From the French press print fabric, cut out a panel that measures 17 x 28 inches (43.2 x 71.1 cm). This piece will be the under apron.

22 Place the coffee cup at the corners and mark the curve of the cup with the water-soluble marker. Cut off the curves. FIG. 12

23 Unfold one side of the cream bias tape and pin it, with right sides facing, to the outer edge of the French press panel. With tan thread on the sewing machine and in the bobbin, stitch the bias tape in place along the bias fold. FIG. 13

24 Along the outer edge of the bias tape, stitch a basting stitch at both curves. Pull on the top thread to cinch in the bias tape to allow it to lay flat. FIG. 14

25 Fold the bias tape to the wrong side of the panel and then stitch it in place close to the bias tape folded edge.

26 With black thread on the sewing machine and in the bobbin, stitch the soutache braid into place right on top of the hem stitching. FIG. 15

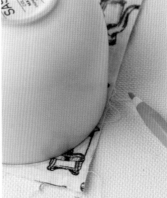

16

17

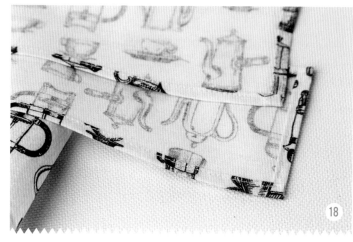

18

27 Fold the under apron in half widthwise and mark the center front at the top. Repeat for the outer apron

28 Pin the outer apron to the under apron, matching center front marks, wrong side of outer apron on right side of under apron. FIG. 16

29 Machine-stitch, using a basting stitch, across the top edge two times. The first row of stitching will be ½ inch (1.3 cm) from the top edge; the second row of stitching will be ¼ inch (6 mm) from the top edge. Do not back-tack at the beginning or at the end of these stitched rows.

30 From the wrong side, gently pull the thread from both of these two rows of stitching, gathering the layers. Continue gathering until the piece measures 15½ inches (39.4 cm). FIG. 17

31 From the French press fabric, cut 2 pieces that measure 3¼ x 36 inches (8.3 x 91.4 cm). These pieces will be the apron ties.

32 Press under one short side and both long sides by ¼ inch (6 mm). Press these sides under another ¼ inch (6 mm). Stitch in place, close to the inner fold, around all three sides. Repeat for the second tie. FIG. 18

33 From the tan linen, cut a panel that measures 6 x 16 inches (15.2 x 40.6 cm). This piece will be the waistband. Press the waistband in half lengthwise, wrong sides facing.

34 From the lightweight interfacing, cut a panel that measures 3 x 16 inches (7.6 x 40.6 cm).

35 Following the manufacturer's directions, fuse the interfacing to the wrong side of one half of the waistband. The top edge of the interfacing should meet the pressed fold.

36 Press the long edge of the linen waistband half without interfacing under to the wrong side by ½ inch (1.3 cm). FIG. 19

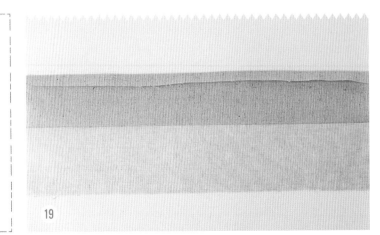

19

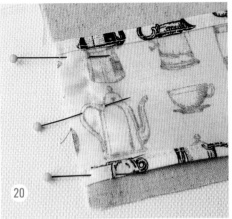

20

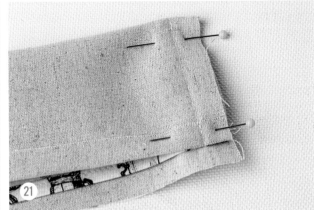

21

37 With right sides facing, pin the raw short edge of the apron tie to the short end of the waistband half that has the interfacing fused to it. The tie should line up with the folded edge and ½ inch (1.3 cm) from the bottom edge. Repeat for the tie at the opposite end. FIG. 20

38 Baste the ties in place with a ¹/₂-inch (1.3-cm) seam allowance at each end.

39 Now fold the right side of the non-interfaced half of the waistband back over the wrong side of the tie, with the folded edge lining up with the edge of the tie, ½ inch (1.3 cm) from the edge. The right sides of the waistband are facing in.

22

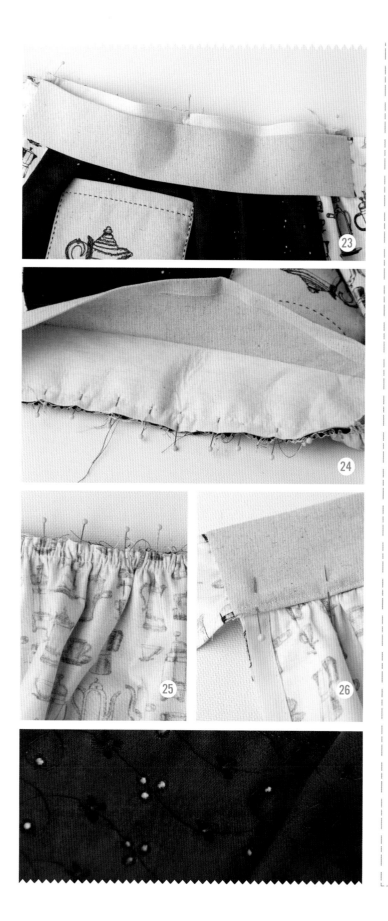

40 Stitch over the basted seam with a ½-inch (1.3-cm) seam allowance. Clip the corners diagonally and turn the waistband right side out. FIGS. 21 & 22

41 Fold the waistband in half width-wise and place a mark at center front. FIG. 23

42 Pin the raw edge of the waistband to the apron, matching them at center front and at both ends of the waistband. Place several pins to keep the gathers from shifting. FIG. 24

43 Stitch the waistband and apron together using a ½-inch (1.3-cm) seam allowance. Be careful to not catch the other half of the waistband while sewing. FIG. 25

44 Turn the waistband right side out and press the seam allowance toward the waistband.

45 Pin and then stitch the waistband in place, close to the folded edge, and lightly press the apron seams. FIG. 26

owl & feather
bookmark

Readers of all ages will love these colorful bookmarks.

what you need

Basic Sewing Kit (page 9)

Owl & Feather Bookmark
template A (page 133)

Turquoise felt, 2¼ x 8 inches
(5.7 x 20.3 cm)

Peach felt, 2¼ x 8 inches
(5.7 x 20.3 cm)

Brown print cotton, 2¼ x 8
inches (5.7 x 20.3 cm)

Brown thread

Brown acrylic paint

Seam ripper

Small paintbrush

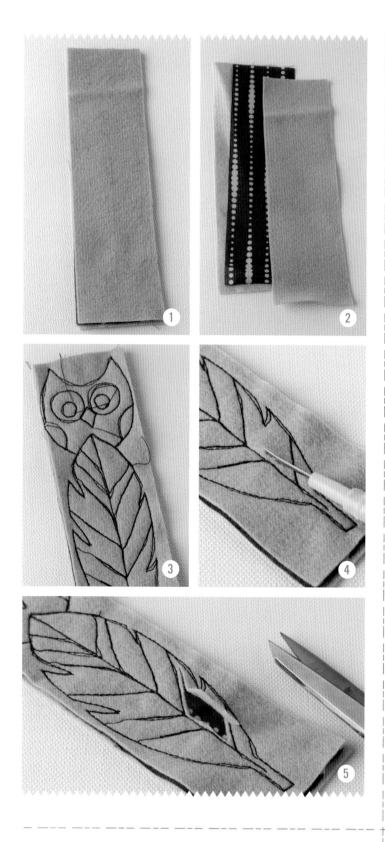

what you do

note: *These instructions are for making the Owl and Feather bookmark, but templates to make different variations are on page (133–134). To make, just follow the basic instructions below, but substitute different felt and cotton fabrics to your liking.*

1 Transfer the image of the owl on a feather (template A) onto the turquoise felt piece. Use wax-free carbon paper to transfer the image to the felt. FIG. 1

2 Lay the brown print cotton on top of the peach felt piece. Place the turquoise piece on top of the print piece. FIG. 2

3 With brown thread on the sewing machine and in the bobbin, free-motion stitch along the transferred lines. Stitch back over the first line of stitching to create a sketchy look. Trim the threads close to the stitching. FIG. 3

4 Insert the seam ripper into a stitched section of the feather and carefully slice about ½ inch (1.3 cm) into the turquoise felt, being careful not to cut through the brown print cotton fabric. FIG. 4

5 Insert the scissors into the slice and carefully cut away the turquoise felt section, ⅛ inch (3 mm) from the stitching, to reveal the brown print cotton fabric. FIG. 5

6 Repeat step 5 several more times on different sections on the feather.

7 Insert the seam ripper into a section of the feather showing brown print cotton fabric and carefully slice the fabric, being careful to not slice into the peach felt.

8 Insert the scissor into the slice and cut away the brown print cotton fabric section, ⅛ inch (3 mm) from the stitching, revealing the peach felt. FIG. 6

9 Repeat step 8 twice more.

10 Insert the seam ripper into the rounded wing section on the face and slice the turquoise felt.

11 Insert the scissor into the slice and cut away the turquoise felt sections.

12 Repeat steps 10 and 11 for the other wing, as well as for the outer eye sections.

13 Insert the seam ripper into the beak section and slice the turquoise felt. Insert the scissors into the slice and cut away the turquoise felt section.

14 Insert the seam ripper into the brown print cotton fabric of the beak and slice the fabric. Insert the scissors into the slice and cut away the brown print fabric to reveal the peach felt.

15 Cut out around the feather and owl shape, ⅛ inch (3 mm) from the outer stitching. FIG. 7

16 Paint the inner eye with the brown acrylic paint. FIG. 8

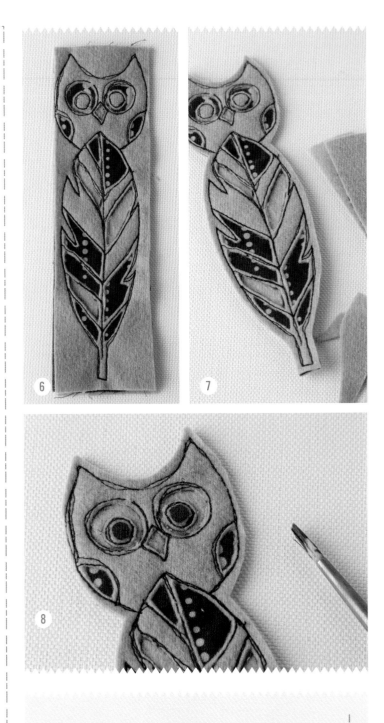

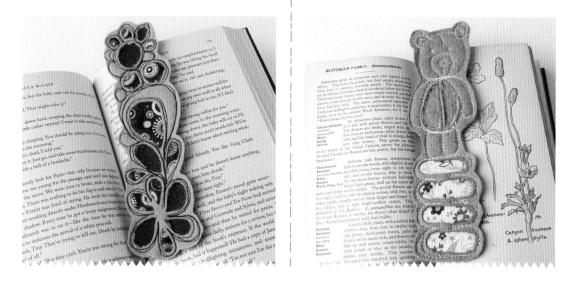

fabric collage bulletin board

Perfect for a dorm room, office or kitchen, this bulletin board will add some excitement to your notes and collectibles.

what you need

Basic Sewing Kit (page 9)

Fabric Collage Bulletin Board templates (page 134-135)

Drill fabric, 24 x 32 inches (61 x 81.3 cm)

Fabric in coordinating colors as follows: 3 or 4 prints in gray and beige, 3 or 4 prints in orange, 3 or 4 prints in pink and fuchsia, 2 or 3 prints in lime green, 3 or 4 prints in aqua and teal **note:** *No more than ¼ yard (22.9 cm) of any of these prints is needed, and in some cases, only scraps were used.*

2 pieces of white cotton batting, each 23½ x 31½ inches (59.7 x 80 cm)

Thread in gray, orange, and another color of your choice

Acrylic paint in white, aqua, gray, orange and lime green

Frame, 24 x 28 inches (61 x 71.1 cm)

⅛-inch- (3-mm-) thick cork, 23½ x 31½ inches (59.7 x 80 cm)

Water-soluble fabric marker

Permanent spray adhesive

Baby wipes or a soft damp cloth

Small paintbrush

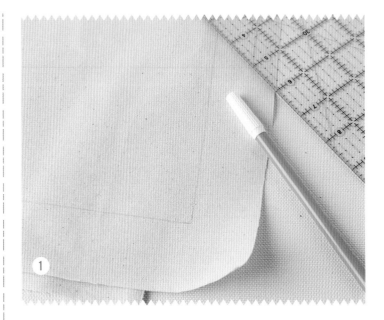

what you do

1 If your drill fabric has not been prewashed, set your iron to Cotton and thoroughly steam the fabric. Because this panel will get wet from the paint, steaming it beforehand will keep the fabric from shrinking and buckling once the paint is dry.

2 Using the quilters' see-through ruler and water-soluble fabric marker, mark around the perimeter of the fabric 1¾ inches (4.4 cm) from the cut edges. FIG. 1

3 Starting with the gray and beige fabrics, cut six or seven rectangles, squares, and various geometric shapes approximately 6 x 6 inches (15.2 x 15.2 cm). The sizes can vary and the cuts can be quick; some can even have a slanted edge.

4 Arrange these pieces on the drill fabric, evenly spaced and running horizontally or vertically. Place some of the pieces on the marked line at the edge.

5 Using the orange fabrics, cut rectangles and various geometric shapes approximately 5 x 3 inches (12.7 x 7.6 cm).

6 Arrange these pieces on the drill fabric, overlapping some of the existing gray and beige pieces. Line the pieces up so that they are running horizontally or vertically.

7 Using the pink and fuchsia fabrics, cut rectangles and various geometric shapes approximately 5 x 3 inches (12.7 x 7.6 cm).

8 Arrange these pieces on the drill fabric, overlapping some of the existing pieces. Line the pieces up so that they are running horizontally or vertically.

9 Using the lime green and aqua fabrics, cut rectangles and various geometric shapes approximately 5 x 3 inches (12.7 x 7.6 cm).

10 Arrange these pieces on the drill fabric, overlapping some of the existing pieces. Line the pieces up so that they are running horizontally or vertically and filling in most of the exposed drill fabric.

11 Using the gray and beige fabrics, cut small rectangles to fill in the last little gaps between fabrics.

12 Stand back a bit, view the panel from a distance, and decide if there is a particular area on the panel where there is too much color or not enough, or if there seems to be one fabric that pops out too much. Rearrange the pieces to your liking. **note:** *It's okay to have one or two pieces that do draw your eye into the panel.* FIG. 2

13 Pin all the fabric pieces down and lightly iron the piece to set the pieces in place.

14 With gray thread on the sewing machine and any color you wish in the bobbin, free-motion stitch around the cut edge of each piece of fabric. **note:** *This is a great project to use up half-full bobbins of thread.* Free-motion stitch in straight lines, wavy lines, loops, scallops, and circles. Free-motion stitch small flowers, stems, and pods. FIG. 3

15 Trace the large feather, small feather, flower, and large flowers templates provided for the project onto paper and then cut them out. Place these shapes onto the fabric collage and, using a water-soluble marker, trace around the shapes. FIG. 4

16 With orange thread on the sewing machine, free-motion stitch the traced motifs. Stitch around the shapes a couple times to get that sketchy look. FIGS. 5 & 6

17 Free-motion stitch small triangles, circles, stems, and small flowers. (Flip the panel over to see how cute all the free-motion stitched shapes are!) Trim the threads close to the stitching. FIG. 7

18 Using white paint and a small paintbrush, paint around the free-motion-stitched feathers, flowers, and scallops. Start by painting close to the stitching line with a good amount of paint on the brush and then feather the paint out as you get farther away from the stitching. Use a baby wipe or a soft damp cloth to help blend the paint into the fabric. **note:** *Thin out the paint with just a few drops of water to help the paint absorb into fabric.* FIGS. 8 & 9

19 Paint some free-motion-stitched shapes with the aqua, orange, and lime green paints.

20 Paint the center of the big flower orange, and then paint small portions of the petals with the gray paint. FIG. 10

21 Take the back panel off the frame and discard any glass.

22 Using spray adhesive, adhere the cork panel to the inside of the frame's backboard. Smooth out the cork to make sure that it is securely attached to the board. The cork is slightly smaller than the backboard, so make sure that it is centered in the backboard. FIG. 11

23 Lightly spray the cork with spray adhesive and place one layer of batting on top of the cork. Smooth out the batting to make sure it is evenly adhered to the cork. Repeat for the other piece of batting. FIG. 12

24 Lightly spray the wrong side of the stitched collage panel with spray adhesive. Carefully center and place the batting side of the backboard onto the collage panel. FIG. 13 Flip the board over and smooth out the collage panel, making sure that it is secured to the batting.

25 Place the collage panel into the frame. This will be snug, but it will fit! FIG. 14

26 Roll the excess fabric from the panel toward the board and swing the frame tabs into place, securing the backboard into the frame. FIG. 15

cloud & elephant
bib and burp cloth

Tiny elephants and clouds add a sweet touch for the little one.

what you need

Basic Sewing Kit (page 9)

Cloud & Elephant Bib and Burp Cloth templates A–D (page 136)

½ yard (45.7 cm) of elephant print flannel

⅛ yard (11.4 cm) of blue-and-white striped cotton fabric

⅛ yard (11.4 cm) of gray-and-white zigzag-print flannel

1 yard (91.4 cm) of light blue terry cloth

⅓ yard (30.5 cm) of cloud print flannel

23 inches (58.4 cm) of white jumbo rickrack

Thread in white and teal

Silver snap fastener

Water-soluble fabric marker

Ruler

Damp cloth

what you do to make the burp cloth

note: *Use a ½-inch (1.3-cm) seam allowance.*

1 Cut a panel from the elephant fabric that measures 13 x 15 inches (33 x 38.1 cm).

2 Cut a strip from the blue-and-white striped fabric that measures 13 x 2½ inches (33 x 6.4 cm).

3 Press the striped-fabric strip in half lengthwise with wrong sides together.

4 Pin, then stitch the strip to the right side of one of the short ends of the elephant print panel. FIG. 1

5 Cut a length of rickrack that measures 13 inches (33 cm).

6 Center the rickrack over the stitching line on the blue-and-white strip and pin. Stitch the rickrack in place down the center. FIG. 2

7 Cut a panel of the gray-and-white zigzag fabric that measures 13 x 4¼ inches (33 x 10.8 cm).

8 Using the water-soluble marker and ruler, draw a line 1¼ inches (3.2 cm) up from the one long edge of the panel cut in step 7. Transfer template A to the panel three times, using a light box or the window method: center the first elephant on the drawn line, then mark the remaining two elephants, also standing on the line, so the trunks and tails are ½ inch (1.3 cm) apart. FIG. 3

9 With right sides facing, pin and then stitch the gray zigzag panel to the elephant panel. Press the seam to one side. FIG. 4

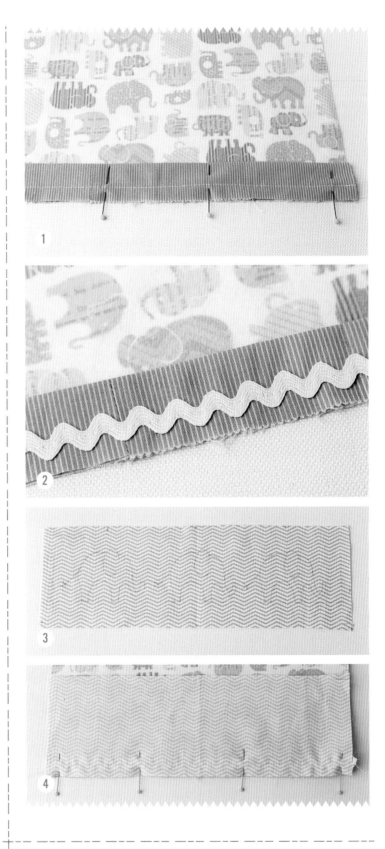

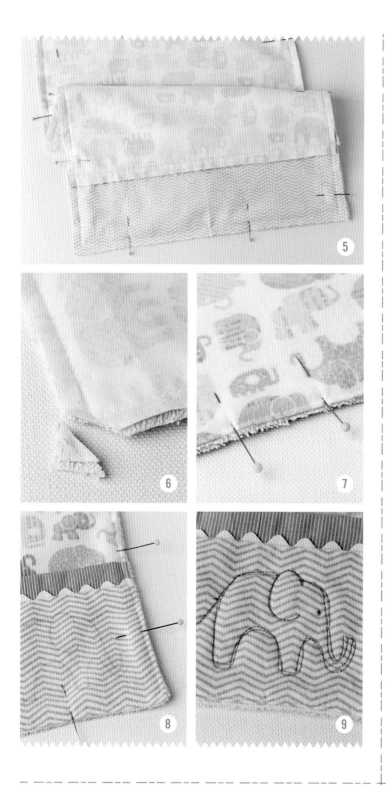

10 From the terry-cloth fabric, cut a panel that measures 13 x 19 inches (33 x 48.3 cm).

11 Place the stitched flannel panel on top of the terry cloth panel, right sides together. Pin around the outer edge. Back-tacking at the start and the finish of the seam, stitch around the perimeter, starting at one of the short ends and pivoting at the four corners. Leave a 4-inch (10.2-cm) opening on the short end for turning. FIG. 5

12 Trim the corners at a diagonal and then turn the burp cloth right side out through the unstitched 4-inch (10.2-cm) opening. FIG. 6

13 Lightly press the burp cloth around the perimeter, poking the corners out with a pin. Press the seam allowance in at the opening and machine-stitch the opening close to the folds. FIG. 7

14 Stitch around the perimeter of the burp cloth, ⅛ inch (3 mm) from the outer edges. FIG. 8

15 With teal thread on the sewing machine and in the bobbin, free-motion stitch the elephants. Stitch back over the first stitching lines to get that sketchy look. FIG. 9

16 Use a damp cloth to erase the water-soluble lines. Trim the threads close to the stitching.

what you do to make the bib

note: *Use a ¼-inch (6-mm) seam allowance.*

1 Using template D, cut one piece from the gray-and-white zigzag flannel. Transfer all markings to the right side of the fabric.

2 Using template B, cut one piece from the cloud flannel fabric. Transfer all the markings to the right side of the fabric.

3 Using template C, cut one piece from the blue-and-white striped fabric. Transfer all the markings to the right side of the fabric.

4 Using the water-soluble marker and ruler, draw a line 1¼ inches (3.2 cm) up from the bottom. Transfer template A to the panel, centering and standing the elephant on the drawn line. FIG. 1

5 Cut a length of rickrack that measures 8¼ inches (21 cm) and pin it to the blue striped strip from step 3 along the side that has the two transferred marks, aligning the bottom edge of the rickrack to the cut edge of the strip. Stitch the rickrack in place down the center. FIG. 2

6 Pin the gray-and-white zigzag piece to the blue striped piece, right sides facing and matching the double transferred marks. Stitch the seam and then lightly press the seam toward the gray-and-white zigzag piece. FIG. 3

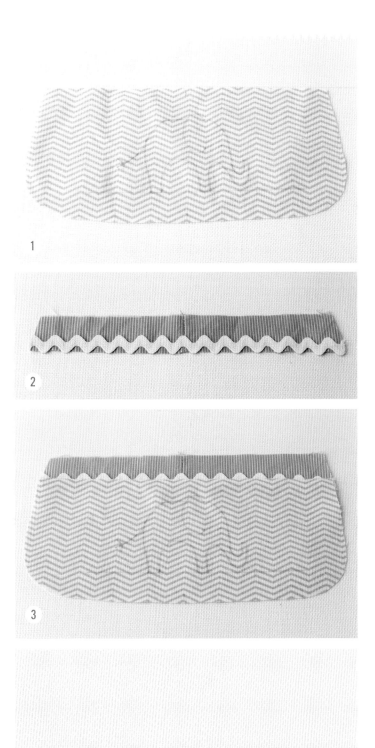

1

2

3

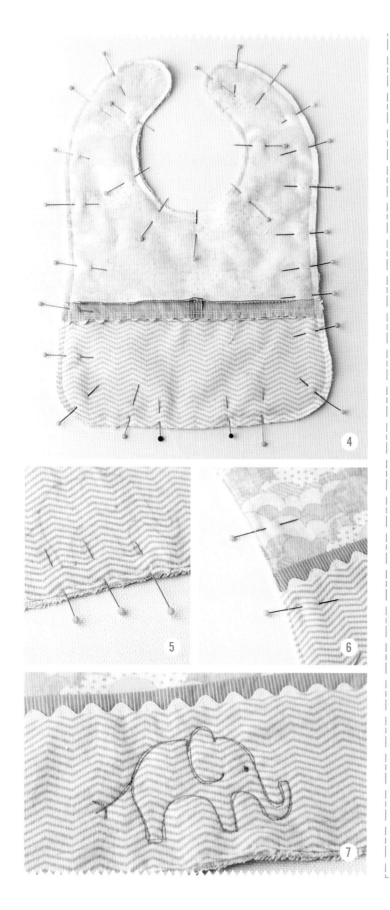

7 Pin the cloud piece to the blue striped piece, matching the single transferred mark. Stitch the seam and then lightly press the seam allowance toward the striped fabric.

8 Place the bib, wrong side facing up, onto the light blue terry cloth. Pin the piece in place and then cut out around the bib, close to the edge. Stitch around the perimeter of the bib. Start stitching at the bottom, straight edge. Back-tacking at the start and the finish of the seam, stitch around the bib leaving a 4-inch (10.2-cm) opening. FIG. 4

9 Turn the bib right side out through the 4-inch (10.2-cm) opening. Press the bib flat, folding the seam allowance in at the opening. Machine-stitch the opening close to the fold. FIG. 5

10 Stitch around the perimeter of the bib ⅛ inch (3 mm) from the outer edges. FIG. 6

11 With teal thread on the sewing machine and in the bobbin, free-motion stitch the elephant. Stitch back over the first stitching to get that sketchy look. FIG. 7

12 Trim the threads close to the stitching.

13 Following the manufacturer's directions set the snap on the bib at the transferred marks.

bespoke clutch

Throw your keys, wallet and favorite lipstick in this perfect carryall.

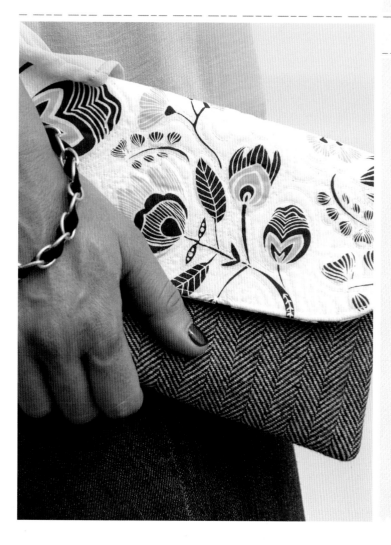

what you need

Basic Sewing Kit (page 9)

Bespoke Clutch templates
A (Body) and B (Flap) (page 137)

¼ yard (22.9 cm) of navy-and-white herringbone wool suiting for the clutch body

¼ yard (22.9 cm) of cotton fabric for the clutch and clutch flap lining

¼ yard (22.9 cm) of cotton print fabric for the clutch flap

¼ yard (22.9 cm) of fusible fleece

Gold magnetic purse snap, ¾ inch (1.9 cm) in diameter

Thread in white and navy blue

11 inches (27.9 cm) of navy blue suede trim, ¼ inch (6 mm) wide

12-inch (30.5-cm) length of gold chain, ½-inch (1.3-cm) links.

Craft knife

Needle-nose pliers

what you do

note: *Use a ¼-inch (6-mm) seam allowance.*

1 Using template A, cut out 2 from the wool herringbone, 2 from the clutch lining, and 2 from the fusible fleece.

2 Transfer the mark for the snap onto the right side of one of the herringbone pieces.

3 Using template B, cut out one from the clutch flap fabric, one from clutch flap lining, and one from fusible fleece. FIG. 1

4 Transfer the mark for the snap onto the right side and the wrong side of the lining piece. FIG. 2

5 Cut out a piece of fusible fleece that measures 1 x 1 inch (2.5 x 2.5 cm). Center the square over the snap mark and, following the manufacturer's directions, adhere it to the wrong side of the clutch flap lining. FIG. 3

6 Following the manufacturer's directions, attach the top half or the male piece of the magnetic snap, centered on the snap mark, on the right side of the clutch flap lining. FIGS. 4 & 5

7 Following the manufacturer's directions, adhere the fusible fleece to the wrong side of the flap fabric and to the wrong side of the navy blue herringbone clutch pieces.

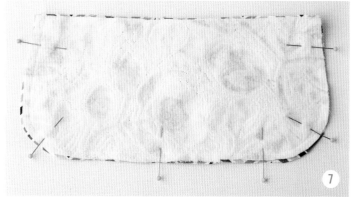

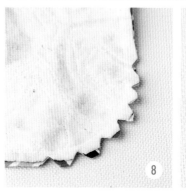

8 With white thread on the sewing machine and in the bobbin, free-motion stitch around the print on the flap piece, filling in the open white space with multiple stitching lines. Trim the threads close to the stitches. FIG. 6

9 With right sides facing, pin the flap lining to the free-motion-stitched flap piece. Back-tacking at the beginning and the end of the seam, stitch the outer curved edge. FIG. 7

10 At the curves, cut small wedge shapes out of the seam allowance, close to the stitched seam, but be careful not to cut through the stitching. FIG. 8

11 Turn the flap right side out and press the flap.

12 Topstitch (page 10) close to the outer curved edge. FIG. 9

13 With right sides facing, pin the herringbone pieces together along the outer curved edge, then stitch, back-tacking at the beginning and the end of the seam. FIG. 10

14 At the curves, cut small wedge shapes out of the seam allowance, close to the stitched seam, but be careful not to cut through the stitching. FIG. 11

15 Turn the piece right side out and press.

16 From the lining fabric, cut a strip that measures 1¼ x 3 inches (3.2 x 7.6 cm).

17 Press the strip in half lengthwise, then fold the outer edges in toward the fold. Fold the strip in half again, lengthwise. Stitch close to the folded edges. FIGS. 12 & 13

18 Fold the strip in half crosswise and pin it to the clutch on the outside at the seam line as shown. FIG. 14

19 Baste the strip in place. This will be the loop that the chain will connect to.

20 With right sides facing, pin the clutch flap to the clutch body, matching the top edges; the loop (step 19) should be on the right side. Stitch the flap to the clutch. FIG. 15

21 With right sides facing, pin the clutch lining together. Back-tacking at the beginning and the end of the seam and leaving a 3-inch (7.6-cm) gap unstitched along the straight edge, stitch the lining along the outer curved edge. Clip the corner near the stitching line. FIGS. 16 & 17

22 Place the herringbone clutch inside the clutch lining with right sides together and pin them together along the opening. FIG. 18

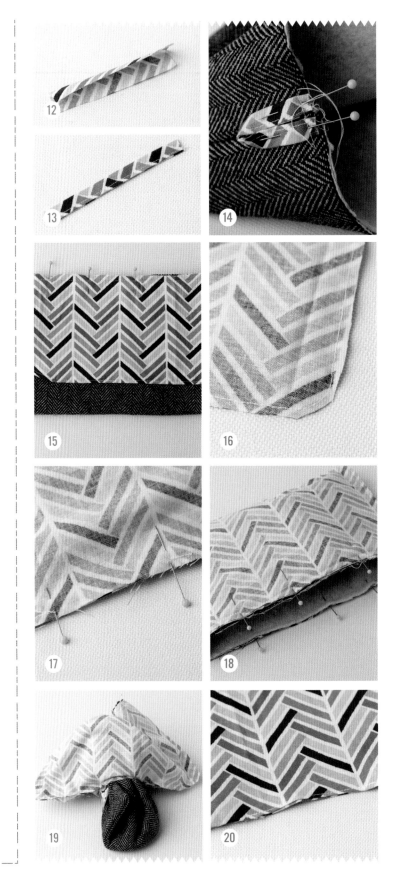

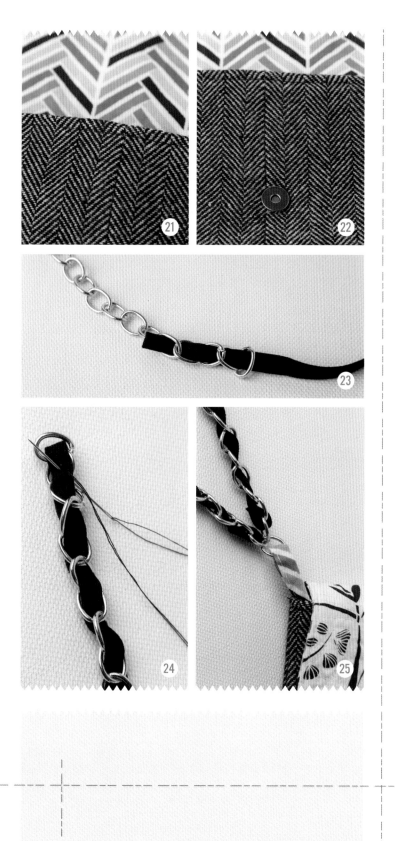

21

22

23

24

25

23 Stitch the seam and then turn the clutch right side out through the 3-inch (7.6-cm) gap in the clutch lining. FIG. 19

24 At the gap in the lining, fold the seam allowance in and then stitch it closed. FIG. 20

25 Push the lining into the clutch and then press the top edge.

26 With navy blue thread on the sewing machine and in the bobbin, topstitch around the top edge of the clutch. FIG. 21

27 Following the manufacturer's directions, attach the bottom half or the female piece of the magnetic snap, centered on the snap mark, on the right side of the clutch. FIG. 22

28 Weave the suede trim in and out of the gold chain. FIG. 23

29 At both ends, fold the trim over by ¼ inch (6 mm) and hand-stitch it around the last chain link. FIG. 24

30 Using needle-nose pliers, open up one link from the gold chain and hook it onto the clutch loop and the opposite end of the chain. FIG. 25

diamond-stitched burlap
chalkboard or mirror frame

This frame adds a personal touch to any space.

what you need

Basic Sewing Kit (page 9)

½ yard (45.7 cm) of gray burlap

½ yard (45.7 cm) of white cotton batting

Black felt, 9 x 11½ inches (22.9 x 29.2 cm)

Thread in black and maroon

Temporary fabric spray adhesive

Water-soluble fabric pen

Wood frame, 9 x 11 inches (22.9 x 27.9 cm)

White chalk fabric pencil

Permanent spray adhesive

Duct tape or white craft glue

Mirror or chalkboard panel

what you do

1 Cut a panel of burlap and one of white cotton batting that each measure 14 x 16 inches (35.6 x 40.6 cm).

2 Place the burlap rectangle on top of the cotton batting. Use temporary spray adhesive to hold these two layers together. FIG. 1

3 Measure 1 inch (2.5 cm) in from the top left corner and the bottom right corner and draw a diagonal line connecting these two points. Repeat for the top right corner and the bottom left corner. FIG. 2

4 With black thread on the sewing machine and in the bobbin, free-motion stitch over the diagonal lines. Stitch another diagonal line on each side of these lines, spacing the lines randomly between ¾ inch (1.9 cm) and 1¼ inches (3.2 cm) apart. **note:** *Having a little wiggly line here and there is a good thing and adds interest to the frame.* FIG. 3

5 Continue stitching the burlap until the entire piece has been diagonally stitched to create diamond shapes. Stitch back over all the stitched lines to give the piece a sketchy look.

6 Fold the stitched burlap panel in half lengthwise and then widthwise and crease lightly. Place pins along these crease lines.

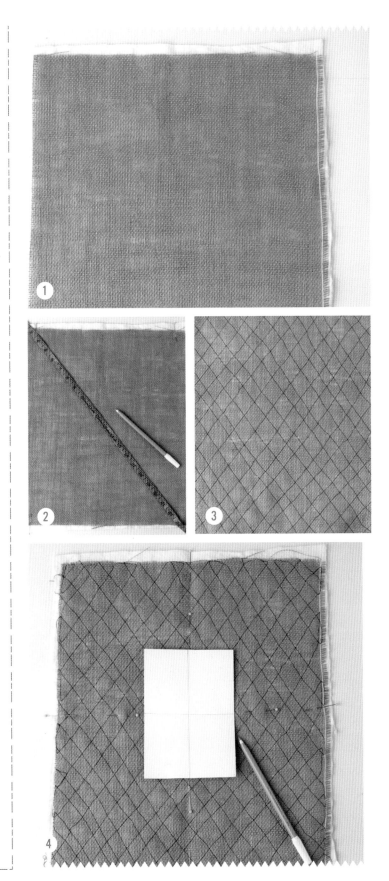

7 Trace the inside opening of the frame onto a piece of paper and then cut out the rectangle.

8 Fold the paper rectangle in half lengthwise and then widthwise. Place marks at the four fold creases.

9 Place the rectangle on top of the burlap panel and match up the crease marks with the pins to find the center of the burlap panel. FIG. 4

10 Using a water-soluble fabric marker, trace around the paper rectangle. FIG. 5

11 Center the frame on the stitched burlap. Using a water-soluble fabric marker, trace around the frame. FIG. 6

12 Lay the burlap piece flat and, with a water-soluble pen, mark diamond shapes that you want to fill in with black stitching. Avoid the area inside the interior marked rectangle. This area will be cut away and never seen. FIG. 7

13 Free-motion stitch inside the marked diamond shapes using black thread on the sewing machine and bobbin. Stitch back and forth over each shape, parallel to the outer stitches. The filled-in diamonds will look like hash marks. FIG. 8

14 Lay the burlap piece flat and now mark diamond shapes that will be filled in with maroon thread. FIG. 9

15 Change the sewing machine so there is maroon thread on the top and in the bobbin. Free-motion stitch back and forth, parallel to the outer stitches, to fill in the selected diamond shapes. FIG. 10

16 Trim the threads close to the stitching.

17 Place the frame on top of the black felt and trace around the perimeter and the inside opening with the white chalk fabric pencil. Cut out around the black felt as well as the inside rectangle. FIG. 11

18 Trim an additional ½ inch (1.3 cm) off the outer edge of the felt. Do not throw this trimmed scrap away.

19 Find the center of the burlap panel and make a little snip with the scissors. Continue cutting at an angle toward all four corners of the traced inside frame opening, stopping ½ inch (1.3 cm) from each corner. FIG. 12

20 Spray the back of the burlap panel with permanent spray adhesive.

21 Place the wood frame onto the sprayed surface and wrap the inside portion of the frame as shown. FIG. 13

22 Fold all the corners onto the wood frame and then cut out a notch as shown to reduce some of the bulk. FIG. 14

23 Fold the sides of the burlap in, the top portion down, and the bottom portion up. FIG. 15

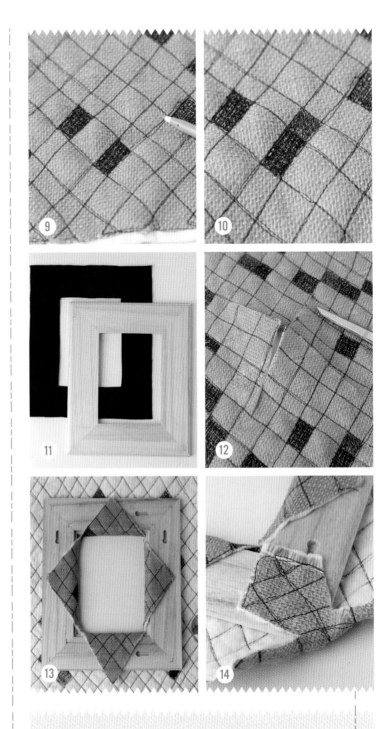

24 With the felt strip that was cut off and saved in step 18, cut lengths that fit in the inside of the frame opening. Spray one side of a black felt strip with permanent spray adhesive and then place it on the back of the frame, covering up the burlap folds and cuts. Repeat with the remaining black felt strips. FIG. 16

25 Using permanent adhesive, spray one side of the black piece created in step 17. Quickly adhere this piece to the back of the frame. FIG. 17

26 Tape or glue the mirror or the chalkboard panel to the back of the frame.

house & home dish towel

Wish new home owners well with
a pretty and useful accessory.

what you need

Basic Sewing Kit (page 9)

House & Home Dish Towel
templates A–L (page 138)

½ yard (45.7 cm) of fusible web

Scraps of cotton print fabrics:

*Light gray print for the house on the left,
5½ x 5½ inches (14 x 14 cm)*

*Black-and-white print for the roof,
5½ x 4 inches (14 x 10.2 cm)*

*Gray for the door and windows,
4½ x 4½ inches (10.2 x 10.2 cm)*

*Red print for the tall house in the
middle, 2½ x 9½ inches (6.4 x 24.1 cm)*

*Gray for the roof, 4 x 4 inches
(10.2 x 10.2 cm)*

*Light gray for the door, 2 x 3 inches
(2.5 x 7.6 cm)*

*Green print for the tree, 4 x 9 inches
(10.2 x 22.9 cm)*

*Red print for the house on the right,
5 x 7 inches (12.7 x 17.8 cm)*

*Dark gray print for the roof, 5 x 6 inches
(12.7 x 15.2 cm)*

*Black-and-white print for the door,
2 x 3 inches (5.1 x 7.6 cm)*

*Off-white for the windows, 4 x 2½ inches
(10.2 x 6.4 cm)*

Thread in black, gray, white,
and red

Water-soluble fabric marker

Dish towel, 18 x 28 inches
(45.7 x 71.1 cm)

Gray jumbo rickrack, 19 inches
(48.3 cm)

Red ball fringe or trim, 19 inches
(48.3 cm)

what you do

1 Trace all the templates onto the paper side of the fusible web, separated by about 1 inch (2.5 cm). Cut the traced shapes about ½ inch (1.3 cm) outside the traced lines.

2 Following the manufacturer's directions, fuse the traced shapes onto the wrong side of the fabric as follows:

Template A onto light gray fabric

Template B onto black-and-white fabric

Templates C and D onto gray fabric

Template E onto red print fabric

Template F onto gray fabric

Template G onto light gray fabric

Template H onto green print fabric

Template I onto red print fabric

Template J onto dark gray print fabric

Template K onto black-and-white fabric

Template L onto off-white fabric (cut 2)
FIG. 1

3 Once the fused pieces have cooled, cut out on the line of the shape and then peel off the paper backing.

4 Using the water-soluble marker, draw a line 1¾ inches (4.4 cm) from the bottom of the dish towel.

5 Arrange the houses, roofs, doors, windows, and the tree on the dish towel. Place all of them on the line drawn in step 4 and, following the manufacturer's directions, fuse the pieces in place. FIG. 2

1

2

6 With black thread on the sewing machine and in the bobbin, free-motion stitch around the fused pieces. Free-motion stitch chimneys, doorknobs, windowpanes, scallops on the edge of the roof, and leaves on the tree and falling off. **note:** *The fabric used for the house on the left happened to have birds in the print, so I did plan to have one bird in the perfect place so that when the door was fused onto the house it would look like the bird is sitting on the door frame. If your fabric does not have birds on it you can always free-motion stitch a bird sitting on the doorframe by just looking at this bird as an example.* FIGS. 3-7

7 Trim the threads close to the stitching. Lightly press the fused and stitched pieces.

8 Turn under the ends of the rickrack by ½ inch (1.3 cm).

9 Pin the rickrack to the dish towel, 1/2 inch (1.3 cm) up from the bottom. With gray thread on the sewing machine and white thread in the bobbin, stitch the rickrack in place down the center.

10 Turn under the ends of the red ball fringe by ½ inch (1.3 cm).

11 Pin the trim to the back of the dish towel at the bottom. With white thread on the sewing machine and red thread in the bobbin, stitch it in place, close to the bottom edge of the dish towel. FIG. 8

felt heart ornament

These felt ornaments add a touch of warmth wherever you place them.

what you need

Basic Sewing Kit (page 9)

Heart template (page 139)

Scrap of white cotton batting, 3 x 4¾ inches (7.6 x 12 cm)

Scrap of gray burlap, 3¾ x 5½ inches (9.5 x 14 cm)

Scrap of dark gray wool, 3 x 4½ inches (7.6 x 11.4 cm)

Scrap of pink houndstooth wool, 2 x 4 inches (5.1 x 10.2 cm)

Scrap of dark red wool, 1¾ x 2¼ inches (4.4 x 5.7 cm)

Thread in white and black

7 inches (17.8 cm) of black rayon ribbon, ½ inch (1.3 cm) wide

Page of book text

Matte Mod Podge

Sheet of white card stock

Spray adhesive

12-inch (30.5 cm) length of steel wire

1 black mini square brad

Craft knife

Needle-nose pliers

what you do

note: *These instructions are for making the Heart Ornament, but templates to make different variations are on page 139. To make, just follow the basic instructions below, substituting different felt and wool fabrics to your liking. For the burlap and felt pieces, the size is the same as for the heart ornament; just the colors have been changed to add a variety. Follow the colors I use, or choose your own color combinations.*

1 Copy the heart template onto a piece of paper and then cut out the heart.

2 Trace the heart onto the sheet of book text. Using a craft knife and self-healing cutting mat, cut out the heart.

3 Apply a generous amount of Mod Podge to the white card stock and then place the book text on top. Apply more Mod Podge to the top of the book text. Set aside to dry.

4 Using the craft knife and self-healing cutting mat, cut out the heart shape about 1/16 inch (1.6 mm) from the edge of the book text heart, leaving a small rim of white showing. FIG. 1

5 Tear or cut the book text so that the panel measures approximately 2 1/4 x 3 inches (5.7 x 7.6 cm).

6 Using spray adhesive, attach the cotton batting to the gray burlap, then adhere the dark gray wool to the cotton batting. Next use spray adhesive to attach the pink houndstooth panel to the dark gray wool, (FIG. 2) and adhere the dark red panel to the pink houndstooth wool.

7 Using spray adhesive, adhere the text panel over the dark red wool. FIG. 3

8 With white thread on the sewing machine and in the bobbin, free-motion stitch around all wool panels to keep them in place.

9 Change the sewing machine thread and the bobbin thread to black.

10 Free-motion stitch around the heart and around the perimeter of the text panel. Stitch a few little perpendicular lines to the top and bottom of the text panel and lower right side of the heart.

11 Trim the threads close to the stitching.

12 Poke the end of the wire into the top left corner of the stitched panel. Curl the wire back using the pliers and secure in place. Curl the ends for decoration.

13 Gently bend the wire and then poke the other end of the wire into the top right-hand corner of the stitched panel. Curl the wire back using the pliers and secure in place. Curl the ends for decoration.

14 Add one small square brad to the heart in the upper right corner. Tie the black rayon ribbon on the wire. FIG. 4

note: *Templates are provided to make heart, tree, star and snowman felt ornaments. (see page 139)*

floating framed photo

Frames not only showcase your loved ones or recent vacations, they're great accessories in your home. Try this personalized floating frame as your next addition.

what you need

Basic Sewing Kit (page 9)

Photo

Transparency sheet

Thread in red and black

Acrylic paint in red and white

Double-stick tape

Clear cellophane tape

Sheet of gray card stock,
6 x 8½ inches (15.2 x 21.6 cm)

Sandpaper, 100 or medium grit

Paintbrush

Craft knife

what you do

1 Trim the photo to measure 2¼ x 3¾ inches (5.7 x 9.5 cm).

2 Cut two panels from the transparency sheet that measure 3½ x 5 inches (8.9 x 12.7 cm) each. FIG.1

3 Lightly sand the outer edges of one of the transparency panels. FIG. 2

4 With red thread on the sewing machine and in the bobbin, free-motion stitch a heart shape on the photo. Stitch the heart a few times to get that sketchy look. Paint the heart red. FIG. 3

5 Center and sandwich the photo between the two transparency panels. Use a small piece of double-stick tape to keep the photo in place. FIG. 4

6 To create the rectangle cutout on the gray card-stock panel, mark a line 2 inches (5.1 cm) up from the bottom, 2 inches (5.1 cm) down from the top, and 1⅜ inches (3.5 cm) in from both sides on the back of the gray card stock.

7 Cut out the rectangle using the craft knife and self-healing cutting mat.

8 From the back, tape the transparency to the card, centered over the cutout. FIG. 5

9 With black thread on the sewing machine and in the bobbin, free-motion stitch around the card stock and onto the transparency. Stitch back over your first lines of stitching, purposefully extending the stitching beyond them. Trim the threads close to the stitching. FIG. 6

10 Paint selected areas with the white paint. FIG. 7

floral-painted tablet cover

Tablet covers make great gifts.
Protect your device with free-stitched flowers.

what you need

Basic Sewing Kit (page 9)

Floral-Painted Tablet Cover templates A–E (page 139)

¼ yard (22.9 cm) of white linen

Scraps of fuchsia print fabric

Gray dot fabric

Teal text fabric

Pink print fabric

Orange print fabric

Gray print fabric for the lining

2 panels of fusible fleece that measure 9¼ x 11¼ inches (23.5 x 28.5 cm)

Thread in orange, white, fuchsia, gray, teal, and pink

Large orange button, 1 inch (2.5 cm) in diameter

Water-soluble fabric marker

Fabric glue stick

Acrylic paints in orange, fuchsia, teal, and white

Small paintbrush

what you do

note: *These instructions are for making a tablet cover measuring 8½ x 10 inches (21.6 x 25.4 cm), but sizing can be adjusted to fit your individual tablet.*

1 Cut a panel of white linen that measures approximately 7 x 9 inches (17.8 x 22.9 cm).

2 Trace floral template A onto a sheet of paper.

3 Transfer the floral design of template A onto the white linen panel using a light box and water-soluble fabric marker (page 13).

4 With orange thread on the sewing machine and in the bobbin, free-motion stitch the large flower in orange. Stitch back over your first line of stitching to give the flower a sketchy look. FIG. 1

5 With teal thread on the sewing machine and gray thread in the bobbin, free-motion stitch the teal flowers as shown in photo on page 72. Stitch back over the first line of stitching to give the flower a sketchy look.

6 Using template E, cut out the orange print flower center for the fuchsia and teal flower on the left, then adhere it to the flower using the glue stick.

7 Change the machine thread to fuchsia and the bobbin thread to light gray and then free-motion stitch the flower on the left and the flower in the middle as shown in photo on page 72. Free-motion stitch scallops on the flat edge of the orange print flower center (step 6) and then add stamens coming from between the scallops. FIG. 2

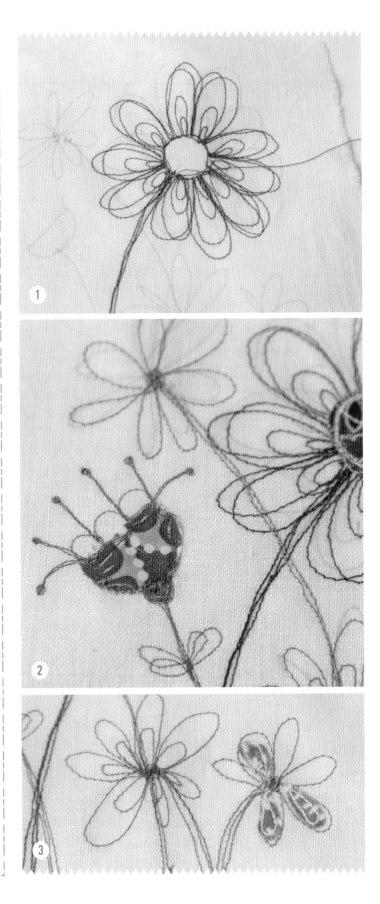

8 Cut out template B from the fuchsia scrap and, using the glue stick, adhere the fabric to the center of the orange flower.

9 Using template C, cut out 1 gray dot petal and, using the glue stick, adhere the large petal on the tall teal stitched flower.

10 Using template D, cut out 7 gray dot petals and, using the glue stick, adhere them to the small petals on the tall teal stitched flower and the short teal stitched flower.

11 Change the machine and the bobbin thread to white and then free-motion stitch around the fuchsia-fabric center several times and then into the center of the circle. Free-motion stitch around all the gray dot petals. FIGS. 3-5

12 Cut a panel from the gray dot fabric that measure 5¾ x 1½ inches (14.6 x 3.8 cm).

13 With the fuchsia thread on the sewing machine and gray thread in the bobbin, free-motion stitch this panel to the bottom right portion of the white linen. **note:** *This piece does not go across the entire bottom portion. There will be a ¾ inch (1.9 cm) gap on the left where the white main fabric is seen.*

14 With fuchsia thread on the sewing machine and gray thread in the bobbin, free-motion stitch small twigs coming up from the gray panel and then add small scallops on the gray panel and on the main white fabric.

15 With teal thread on the sewing machine and gray thread in the bobbin, free-motion stitch large twigs coming up from the gray panel and then onto the main white fabric. FIG. 6

16 Trim the threads close to the stitching.

17 Paint the petals and stem of the orange-stitched flower with orange and fuchsia paints as shown, then paint the teal-stitched flower petals and stems teal.

18 Paint the center fuchsia-stitched flower petals with fuchsia paint and the stem orange.

19 Paint the left-hand fuchsia-stitched flower stem and leaves fuchsia. Paint inside the fuchsia scallops with teal paint. FIG. 7

20 Paint inside the scallops that are on the white linen and the gray dot fabric. Use white paint for the scallops on the gray fabric and orange and fuchsia for the scallops on the white linen. FIG. 8

21 Using the self-healing mat, rotary cutter, and see-through quilters' ruler, trim the white linen panel to measure 6½ x 8¾ inches (16.5 x 22.2 cm). FIG. 9

22 Cut a strip from the gray dot fabric that measures 1½ x 8¾ inches (3.8 x 22.2 cm). With white thread on the sewing machine and in the bobbin, stitch this panel to the right-hand side of the white linen panel with a ¼-inch (6-mm) seam allowance and right sides facing. Press the seam allowance toward the gray dot fabric. FIG. 10

23 Cut a strip from the orange print fabric that measures 1½ x 7⅜ inches (3.8 x 18.7 cm). Stitch this panel to the top of the white linen panel with a ¼-inch (6-mm) seam allowance and right sides facing. Press the seam allowance toward the orange print fabric. FIG. 11

24 Cut a strip from the teal text fabric that measures 2¼ x 9¾ inches (5.7 x 24.8 cm). Stitch this panel to the left-hand side of the white linen panel with a ¼-inch (6-mm) seam allowance and right sides facing. Press the seam allowance toward the teal text fabric. FIG. 12

25 Cut a strip from the pink print fabric that measures 1⅞ x 9 inches (4.8 x 22.9 cm). Stitch this panel to the bottom of the white linen panel, using a ¼-inch (6-mm) seam allowance and with right sides facing. Press the seam allowance toward the orange print fabric. FIG. 13

26 For the back, cut one piece from the pink print fabric and two from the fusible fleece that measure 9¼ x 11¼ inches (23.5 x 28.6 cm) each.

27 Following the manufacturer's directions, fuse the fleece to the wrong side of the white linen panel and the back pink print panel. FIG. 14

28 With pink thread on the sewing machine and pink thread in the bobbin, free-motion stitch scallops onto the teal text fabric, the white linen, and the gray-dot fabric. FIG. 15

29 Paint the inside area of the teal and gray scallops with white paint and the insides of the white scallops with fuchsia and orange paint. FIG. 16

30 Cut two pieces for the lining from the larger gray dot fabric that measure 10¼ x 11¼ inches (26 x 28.6 cm) each. Mark the center along one of the long edges. This mark indicates where the closure loop will be sewn.

31 From the teal text fabric, cut a strip of fabric that measures 1 x 4¾ inches (2.5 x 12 cm).

32 Press the strip in half lengthwise and then press the outer cut edges into the pressed edge. Stitch close to both folded edges. FIG. 17

33 Fold the strip in half to form a loop and pin it to the lining at the center mark made in step 30. Baste the loop in place. Make sure that the loop is facing in toward the lining.

34 With right sides facing, pin the two lining pieces together. Back-tacking at the beginning and the end of all seams, stitch the pieces together, leaving both the long edge where the closure loop has been basted and a portion of the opposite long edge unstitched. Place double pins along this edge to help remind you not to stitch this portion. This opening in the seam will allow you to turn the tablet cover right side out. FIG. 18

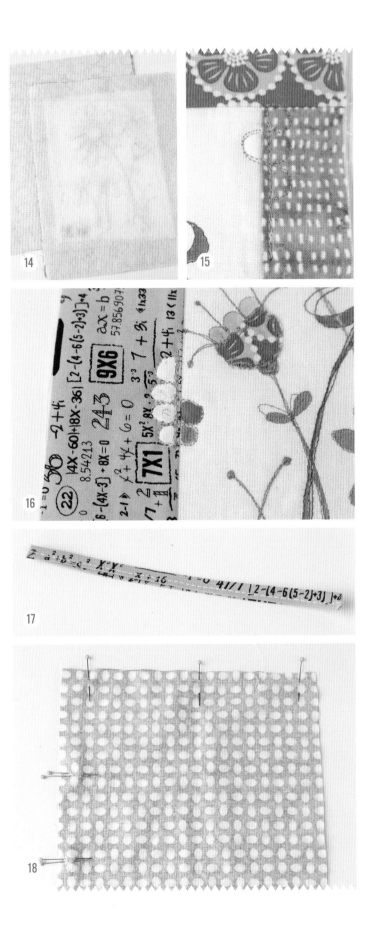

14

15

16

17

18

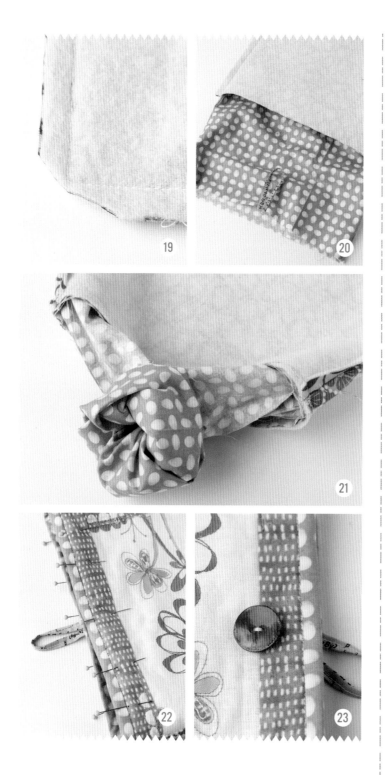

35 Turn the lining right side out.

36 With right sides facing, pin and then stitch the front white linen panel to the back panel using a ¼-inch (6-mm) seam allowance and pivoting at the corners.

37 Trim the corners diagonally close to the stitching. FIG. 19

38 Slip the lining into the outer tablet cover, right sides facing, and pin in place, matching the side seams. Open up the side seams of the lining and the outer tablet cover and pin them in place. Make sure that the closure loop is facing the back portion of the outer tablet cover. Stitch in place using a ¼-inch (6-mm) seam allowance. FIG. 20

39 Turn the tablet cover right side out through the opening in the lining. FIG. 21

40 Turn the seam allowance in at the lining opening and machine-stitch it closed at the folded edges.

41 Push the lining into the tablet cover, allowing the top edge of the lining to roll toward the outside. Pin, then machine-stitch around the opening, in the ditch, or right in the seam line. This stitching will prevent the lining from rolling to the outside. FIG. 22

42 Place the tablet into the cover and flip the closure loop to the front and mark with the water-soluble pen where the button needs to be stitched.

43 Remove the tablet and then hand-stitch the button in place. FIG. 23

little cloth buckets

These buckets are the perfect addition to any space.
Store pens, loose change, or jewelry!

tall little bucket

measures 7¼ inches (18.4 cm) high

what you need

Basic Sewing Kit (page 9)

¼ yard (22.9 cm) of heavy
fusible interfacing

Canvas fabric, 5½ x 5½ inches
(14 x 14 cm)

⅛ yard (11.4 cm) each of
coordinating aqua, light blue,
and navy fabrics (2 different
aqua fabrics)

3½ inches (8.9 cm) of printed
twill tape, ¾ inch (1.9 cm) wide

Thread in aqua, tan, and
navy blue

White cotton fabric for
underlining, 14½ x 9 inches

White cotton fabric for lining,
14 x 11½ inches (35.6 x 29.2 cm)

15 inches (38.1 cm) of white
single-fold bias binding

Water-soluble fabric marker

Circular object, about 4¼ inches
(10.8 cm) in diameter

Temporary spray adhesive

what you do

note: *Use a ¼-inch (6-mm) seam allowance.*

1 Trace a lid or something round onto the fusible interfacing using a water-soluble fabric marker. For this bucket, the circle is 4¼ inches (10.8 cm) in diameter. FIG. 1

2 Cut out the circle and place it onto the canvas, glue side down. Following the manufacturer's instructions, fuse the circle to the canvas, then cut the canvas ⅓ inch (8.4 mm) outside the edge of the interfacing.

3 From one of the aqua fabrics, cut a piece that measures 14 x 3¼ inches (35.6 x 8.3 cm).

4 Measure 6½ inches (16.5 cm) in from the right-hand side and make a mark with the water-soluble fabric marker.

5 Center the printed twill tape on the mark made in step 4. With navy blue thread on the sewing machine and in the bobbin, stitch the outer edges of the twill tape with a decorative feather machine stitch. FIG. 2 & 3

6 From the light blue fabric, cut a piece that measures 14 x 1⅜ inches (35.6 x 3.5 cm).

7 With white thread on the sewing machine and in the bobbin, and with right sides facing, stitch these two panels together on one long side. Press the seam allowance toward the light blue fabric.

8 From the navy blue fabric, cut a piece that measures 14 x 2½ inches (35.6 x 6.4 cm).

9 With right sides facing, stitch this piece to the light blue piece on one long side. Press the seam allowance toward the navy fabric.

10 With aqua thread on the sewing machine and in the bobbin, free-motion stitch wavy lines on the light blue fabric. Change the sewing machine thread to tan and free-motion stitch a few more wavy lines. Repeat the stitching with navy blue thread. Trim the threads close to the stitching. FIG. 4

11 From one of the aqua fabrics, cut a piece that measures 14 x 3¼ inches (35.6 x 8.3 cm).

12 With right sides facing, stitch this piece to the navy piece on one long side. This aqua strip is the top of the bucket. FIG. 5

13 Press the seam allowance toward the aqua strip.

14 Place this pieced panel on the heavy fusible interfacing and cut out the interfacing panel.

15 Following the manufacturer's directions, fuse the interfacing to the wrong side of pieced panel.

16 From the right side, topstitch ¹⁄₁₆ inch (1.6 mm) from the seam, on the right side.

17 Place the interfaced side of the pieced panel onto the underlining. Align the top edges. Using temporary spray adhesive, adhere the pieces together. Now place this piece on the wrong side of the lining. Pin all three layers together. **note:** *The white lining will hang down beyond the pieced outer bucket edge by about 2½ inches (6.3 cm).* FIG. 6

18 Bind the top edge of the pieced bucket with the white single-fold binding. Stitch the binding in place using the feather machine stitch and aqua thread.

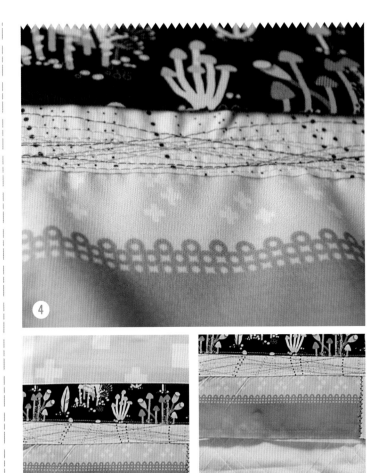

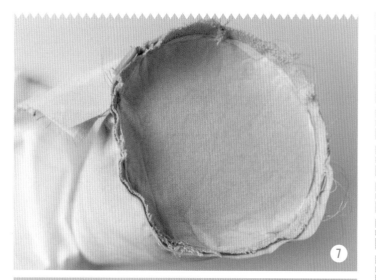

19 Pin the pieced bucket to the canvas bottom. Start pinning the bucket to the canvas ¼ inch (6 mm) from the side of the bucket panel. Work your way around the canvas until you arrive at the beginning, ending ¼ inch (6 mm) from the opposite side. Stitch the piece in place starting the stitching ¼ inch (6 mm) from the bucket side and ending ¼ inch (6 mm) from the opposite bucket side. Make sure you are stitching the pieced bucket with the underlining and not catching the lining piece. FIG. 7

20 Pin the back seam of the bucket, right side facing and the lining and then stitch the side seam.

21 Turn the bucket right side out and place the lining on a flat surface. Flatten the lining at the end, fold the sides in by 2 inches (5.1 cm), and then fold the top edge under Turn under ½ inch (1.3 cm) each time. Stitch in place with two rows of stitching. FIG. 8

22 Push the lining to the inside of the bucket. Roll the top edge of the bucket to the inside by 1 inch (2.5 cm). Stitch the folded edge in place, ½ inch (1.3 cm) from the top edge. FIG. 9

short & skinny little bucket
measures 5 inches (12.7 cm) tall

what you need

Basic Sewing Kit (page 9)

⅛ yard (11.4 cm) of heavy fusible interfacing

Canvas fabric, 4½ x 4½ inches (11.4 x 11.4 cm)

⅛ yard (11.4 cm) each of coordinating aqua, navy, and off-white fabrics (2 different aqua fabrics)

Thread in aqua and light green

White cotton fabric for lining, 10¾ x 8¾ inches (27.3 x 22.2 cm)

13 inches (33 cm) of white single-fold bias tape

Piece of red leather, 1 x 1 inch (2.5 x 2.5 cm)

Water-soluble fabric marker

Circular object, about 3¼ inches (8.3 cm) in diameter

White cotton fabric for underlining, 10¾ x 7 inches (27.3 x 17.7 cm)

what you do

note: *Use a ¼-inch (6-mm) seam allowance.*

1 Trace a lid or something round onto the interfacing using a water-soluble fabric marker. For this bucket the circle is 3¼ inches (8.3 cm) in diameter.

2 Cut out the circle and place onto the canvas, glue side down. Following the manufacturer's instructions, fuse the circle to the canvas, then cut out the canvas ⅓ inch (8.4 mm) from the edge of the interfacing.

3 From one of the aqua fabrics, cut a piece that measures 10¾ x 1¾ inches (27.3 x 4.4 cm).

4 From the navy fabric, cut a piece that measures 10¾ x 2¾ inches (27.3 x 7 cm).

5 With white thread on the sewing machine and in the bobbin, and with right sides facing, stitch these two panels together on one long side. Press the seam allowance toward the navy fabric.

6 From one of the aqua fabrics, cut a piece that measures 10¾ x 1¾ inches (27.3 x 4.4 cm).

7 With right sides facing, stitch this piece to the piece stitched in step 5 on one long side of the navy fabric. Press the seam allowance toward the aqua fabric.

8 From the off-white fabric, cut a piece that measures 10¾ x 2 inches (27.3 x 5.1 cm).

9 With right sides facing, stitch this piece to the piece stitched in step 7 on one long side of the aqua fabric. Press the seam allowance toward the off-white fabric.

10 Place this pieced panel, wrongs side facing the glue side of the heavy fusible interfacing and cut out the interfacing panel.

11 Following the manufacturer's directions, fuse the interfacing to the wrong side of the pieced panel.

12 With aqua thread on the sewing machine and in the bobbin, free-motion stitch a scallop pattern across the top edge of the off-white fabric. Change the thread to light green and stitch several times over the first scallop stitch line. Trim the threads close to the stitching.

13 To finish this bucket, follow steps 16–23 from the Tall Little Bucket instructions (pages 82–83). Cut out a small red leather heart and hand-stitch it to the top edge. **note:** *This bucket does not have an interlining so skip over the first part of step 17 on page 82.*

short little bucket

measures 3 inches (7.6 cm) tall

what you need

Basic Sewing Kit (page 9)

⅛ yard (11.4 cm) of heavy fusible interfacing

Canvas fabric, 6 x 6 inches (15.2 x 15.2 cm)

⅛ yard (11.4 cm) each of coordinating aqua, navy, and light blue fabrics

Thread in aqua, tan, and navy blue

White cotton fabric for lining, 14¾ x 6 inches (37.5 x 15.2 cm)

White cotton fabric for underling 14¾ x 4½ inches

13 inches (33 cm) of white single-fold bias tape

Water-soluble fabric marker

Circular object, about 4½ inches (11.4 cm) in diameter

what you do

note: *Use a ¼-inch (6-mm) seam allowance.*

1 Trace a lid or something round onto the interfacing using a water-soluble fabric marker. For this bucket, the circle is 4½ inches (11.4 cm) in diameter.

2 Cut out the circle and place onto the canvas, glue side down. Following the manufacturer's instructions, fuse the circle to the canvas, then cut the canvas ⅓ inch (8.4 mm) outside the edge of the interfacing.

3 From one of the aqua fabrics, cut a piece that measures 5⅝ x 4 inches (14.3 x 10.2 cm).

4 From the navy fabric, cut a piece that measures 2¼ x 4 inches (5.7 x 10.2 cm).

5 Using white thread on the sewing machine and in the bobbin and with right sides facing, stitch these pieces together along the 4-inch (10.2-cm) side. Press the seam allowance toward the aqua fabric.

6 From the light blue fabric, cut a piece that measures 1¾ x 4 inches (4.4 x 10.2 cm).

7 With right sides facing, stitch this piece to the navy piece along the 4-inch (10.2-cm) side. Press the seam allowance toward the navy fabric.

8 From one of the aqua fabrics, cut a piece that measures 3¼ x 4 inches (8.3 x 10.2 cm).

9 With right sides facing, stitch this piece to the light blue piece along the 4-inch (10.2-cm) side. Press the seam allowance toward the aqua fabric.

10 From one of the aqua fabrics, cut a piece that measures 3⅝ x 4 inches (9.2 cm x 10.2 cm).

11 With right sides facing, stitch this piece to the aqua piece along the 4-inch (10.2-cm) side.

12 From the navy fabric, cut a piece that measures 1¾ x 4 inches (4.4 x 10.2 cm).

13 With right sides facing, stitch this piece to the aqua piece along the 4-inch (10.2-cm) side.

14 Place this pieced panel on the heavy fusible interfacing and cut out the interfacing panel.

15 Following the manufacturer's directions, fuse the interfacing to the wrong side of the pieced panel.

16 With aqua thread on the sewing machine and in the bobbin, free-motion stitch wavy lines on the light blue fabric. Change the sewing machine thread to tan and free-motion stitch a few more wavy lines. Repeat the stitching with navy blue thread. Trim the threads close to the stitching.

17 To finish this bucket follow steps 16–23 from the Tall Little Bucket instructions (pages 82–83). note: *This little bucket is stitched to the canvas base with the panels running vertically. Also, this bucket does not have an interlining so skip over the first part of step 17 on page 82.*

wheat & honey
market tote

There's nothing better than an eco-friendly bag to tote all your goodies.

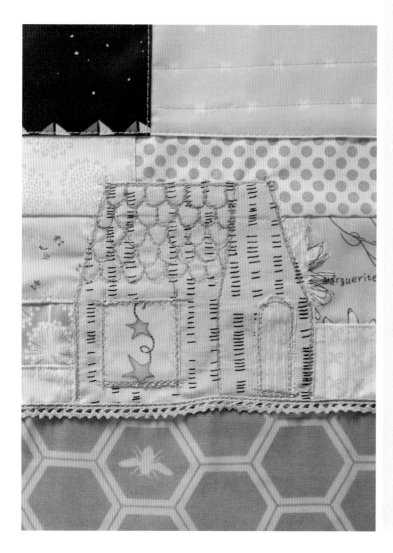

what you need

Basic Sewing Kit (page 9)

Wheat & Honey Market Tote templates A and B (page 140)

⅛ yard (11.4 cm) each of home dec fabrics in gold, brown, off-white, and taupe prints

Printed quilting cotton panel for the bottom lining, 13 x 8 inches (33 x 20.3 cm)

1 yard (91.4 cm) of osnaburg, cut as follows:

> 4 pieces for the side interlining, 8 x 13 inches (20.3 x 33 cm)

> 4 pieces for the front and back interlining, 13 x 13 inches (33 x 33 cm)

Fat quarters of printed quilting cotton and scraps in golden yellow, taupe, navy, and aqua

Linen print fabric for the house on the front of the tote, 6 x 6 inches (15.2 x 15.2 cm)

70 ultra-firm stabilizer, 12 x 7 inches (30.5 x 17.8 cm)

1 yard of fusible interfacing, cut as follows:

> 2 pieces for the sides, 7 x 12 inches (17.8 x 30.5 cm)

> 2 pieces for the front and back, 12 x 12 inches (30.5 x 30.5 cm)

Fusible web, 5 x 5 inches (12.7 x 12.7 cm)

2 yards (1.8 m) of off-white cotton strapping, 1½ inches (3.8 cm) wide, cut into two 1-yard (91.4-cm) pieces

13 inches (33 cm) of decorative aqua cotton trim

Thread in natural and aqua

Temporary fabric spray adhesive

Fabric glue stick

what you do

note: *Use a ½-inch (1.3-cm) seam allowance.*

BOTTOM

1 From the gold home dec fabric, cut a panel that measures 13 x 2½ inches (33 x 6.4 cm). From the brown home dec fabric cut two panels that measure 13 x 3½ inches (33 x 8.9 cm) each.

2 With right sides facing and matching the long sides, pin together one of the brown panels and the gold panel. With natural color thread on the sewing machine and in the bobbin, stitch the seam. FIG. 1

3 With right sides facing and matching the long sides, pin the other brown panel to the opposite side of the gold panel. Stitch the seam. Press the seam allowance toward the brown fabric. FIG. 2

4 Place this stitched panel, right side down, on the work surface. Center the stabilizer panel on top and then place the bottom lining, right side up, on top of the stabilizer. Pin in place. FIG. 3

5 With natural-color thread on the sewing machine and in the bobbin, stitch parallel lines, ¾ inch (1.9 cm) apart, through all three layers, across the entire panel.

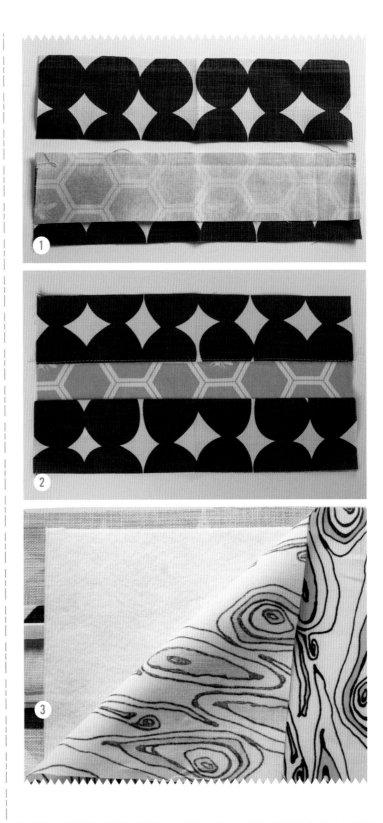

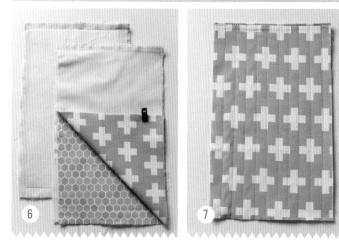

SIDES

6 Following the manufacturer's directions, fuse the interfacing panel that measures 7 x 12 inches (17.8 x 30.5 cm) to the wrong side of one of the osnaburg side interlining panels that measure 8 x 13 inches (20.3 x 33 cm). Repeat for the other side. You will have two side interlining pieces left. FIG. 4

7 From the golden yellow print fat quarter, cut four panels that measure 8 x 13 inches (20.3 x 33 cm). These panels are the outside and inside or lining side panels.

8 Sandwich the side panels as follows: Place 2 gold panels together, right sides facing. Pin to one side, with the wrong side of the gold facing the right side of the interlining that has the fused interfacing on it. To the opposite side, pin the right side of an interlining piece to the wrong side of the gold fabric. Align along one of the short 8-inch (20.3 cm) edges and stitch together through all 4 layers. FIGS. 5 & 6

9 Trim the seam allowance to ¼ inch (6 mm) and then topstitch close to the fold. Pin the panel together and then stitch parallel lines, 1 inch (2.5 cm) apart, through all layers. FIG. 7

10 Repeat steps 6–9 for the other side panel.

BACK AND FRONT

11 From a taupe print fat quarter, cut a panel that measures 9½ x 13 inches (24.1 x 33 cm). Cut another panel from a different fabric that measures 4¾ x 13 inches (12 x 33 cm). Pin these panels together, right sides facing and matching one long edge of each. Stitch together. This will be the back lining. Press the seam allowance open. FIG. 8

12 Place this panel atop an interlining panel. Pin the panels together. FIG. 9

13 Starting at one of the corners, stitch diagonally across the panel to the opposite corner. Repeat for the other corner, creating an X. Now stitch 2 inches (5.1 cm) away from these established stitch lines. Stitch in this manner multiple times until the panel has been completely stitched. FIG. 10

14 From a gold print fat quarter, cut a panel that measures 8¼ x 13 inches (21 x 33 cm). Cut another panel that measures 6 x 13 inches (15.2 x 33 cm). Pin these panels together, right sides facing and matching one long edge of each. Stitch together. FIG. 11

15 Place this panel, wrong side up, on the work surface. Place an interlining panel on top. Pin the panels together.

16 Flip the panel over and topstitch along the fold through all the layers. This panel is the front lining of the tote.

17 To make the outer back panel, spray the center of the 13 x 13-inch (33 x 33-cm) osnaburg interlining with spray adhesive. Now adhere a 12 x 12-inch (30.5 x 30.5-cm) fusible interfacing panel on top of the interlining panel, glue side up.

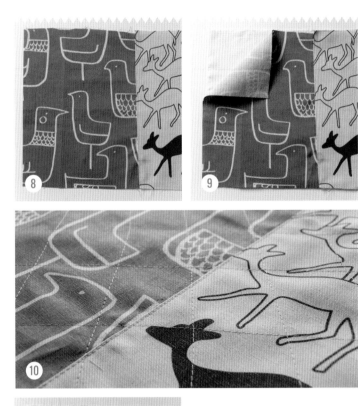

note: *This will allow you to fuse the outer and inner panels together without any gaps or slouching.* FIG. 12

18 Flip this panel over so that the interfacing side is facing down on the work surface.

19 From the taupe quilting cotton fat quarter, cut a square that measures 5 x 5 inches (12.7 x 12.7 cm). Center this square on the interlining panel. Pin in place. FIG. 13

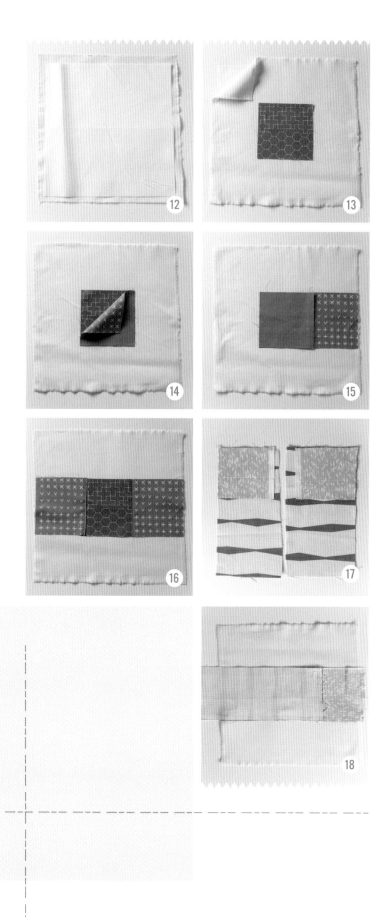

20 Cut a second square from the taupe quilting cotton fat quarter that measures 5 x 5 inches (12.7 x 12.7 cm) and place this piece right side down on top of the centered square. Stitch the right-hand side seam, then press this panel toward the right side. FIG. 14

21 Cut a third square from the taupe quilting cotton fat quarter that measures 5 x 5 inches (12.7 x 12.7 cm) and place this square right side down on top of the centered square. FIG. 15 Stitch this seam along the left-hand side and then press this panel toward the left side. Topstitch close to the two folds. FIG. 16

22 From the off-white and taupe print home dec fabric, cut two panels from each that measure 10 x 5 inches (25.4 x 12.7 cm). From the taupe fat quarter, cut two panels that measure 4½ x 5 inches (11.4 x 12.7 cm) each.

23 With right sides facing and matching the 5-inch (12.7-cm) edge, pin an off-white panel to a taupe panel. Stitch the seam. Repeat for the second taupe and off-white panel. FIG. 17

24 Place this panel on top of the three stitched squares in step 21, right sides facing. FIG. 18 Pin and then stitch the seam; press this panel toward the bottom. Place the second panel on top of the three stitched squares, right sides facing. Pin and then stitch the seam; press this panel toward the top. FIG. 19

25 Using a self-healing cutting mat, see-through quilters' ruler, and rotary cutter, trim the panel to measure 13 x 13 inches (33 x 33 cm). This is the outer back panel. FIG. 20

26 Pin 1 yard (91.4 cm) of cotton strapping to the back panel, placing each end 5 inches (12.7 cm) up from the bottom and 2 inches (5.1 cm) in from the sides. FIG. 21 With natural-color thread stitch the strap in place, 4 inches (10.2 cm) up on both sides, and then stitch an X through the lower portion of the strap.

27 With right sides facing, pin together the inner back panel that has the diagonal stitching and the panel that was created in step 25, matching the top edges. Stitch the seam and then trim it to ¼ inch (6 mm).

28 Flip the panels so that the right sides are out, and then topstitch close to the fold. This panel is the back of the tote.

29 With the second 13 x 13-inch (33 x 33-cm) interlining panel, and 12 x 12-inch (30.5 x 30.5-cm) fusible interfacing panel, repeat step 17.

30 Flip this panel over so that the interfacing side is facing down on the work surface.

31 From the gold, aqua, and navy fat quarters, cut approximately 15 rectangles that measure roughly 8 x 3 inches (20.3 x 7.6 cm) each. Some can be wider and some can be taller.

32 Starting about one-third up from the bottom, pin one of the rectangles to the interlining panel. With right sides together, pin and then stitch a second panel to this panel. Press the rectangle to the side and topstitch the piece in place, close to the fold. Continue in this manner until the top two-thirds of the panel is covered with fabric. FIG. 22

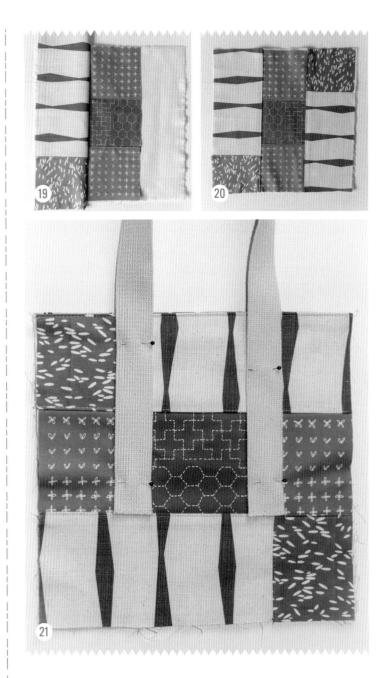

33 Cut a panel from gold print home dec fabric that measures 13 x 4½ inches (33 x 11.4 cm). With right sides facing, pin and then stitch this panel to the patchwork-stitched portion of the tote front created in step 32. Press this panel toward the bottom of the panel.

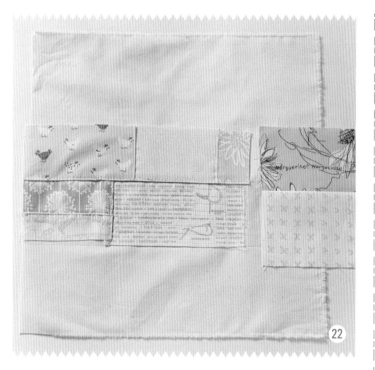

22

40 With aqua thread on the sewing machine and in the bobbin, free-motion stitch around the house. Stitch around the window and the front door. Stitch the roof with a scallop pattern to look like roof tiles. Trim the threads close to the stitching.

41 Stitch the cotton trim over the one-third seam line at the bottom of the house.

42 Pin the remaining 1 yard (91.4 cm) of cotton strapping to the front panel, 5 inches (12.7 cm) up from the bottom and 2 inches (5.1 cm) in from the sides. Stitch the strap in place, 4 inches (10.2 cm) up on both sides, and then stitch an X through the lower portion of the strap.

43 With right sides together, pin together the tote front panel with the panel created in steps 14–16. Stitch the top seam. Flip the panels right side out and then topstitch close to the fold.

ASSEMBLING THE TOTE

44 Pin the side panels to the tote bottom panel, matching the short edges. Stitch in place, starting ½ inch (1.3 cm) from the edge and stopping ½ inch (1.3 cm) from the end.

45 Pin the front and the back panels to the tote bottom panel, matching the bottom edges with the long edge of the bottom panel. Start stitching ½ inch (1.3 cm) in from the edge and stop ½ inch (1.3 cm) from the end.

46 With right sides together, pin all four side seams together. Stitch the seams, then turn the tote right side out.

47 Trim the side seams down to ¼ inch (6 mm), then zigzag-stitch the seam allowance.

34 Trace the house template A to the paper side of the fusible web.

35 Following the manufacturer's directions, adhere the fusible web to the wrong side of the 6 x 6-inch (15.2 x 15.2-cm) linen print panel.

36 When cool, cut out the house and peel off the paper backing.

37 Iron the house onto the tote front panel, centered on the one-third seam line.

38 Cut a square from the off-white quilting cotton that measures 2 x 2 inches (5.1 x 5.1 cm). Use a glue stick to adhere the window to the left portion of the house.

39 Cut out a front door (template B) from the yellow quilting cotton that measures 1 x 2½ inches (2.5 x 6.4 cm). Adhere the door to the right side of the house, using the glue stick.

mod card set

Send this colorful card to a loved one or make a set as a gift.

what you need

Basic Sewing Kit (page 9)

Watercolor paper, 10 x 7 inches (25.4 x 17.8 cm)

White envelope, 5¼ x 7¼ inches (13.3 x 18.4 cm)

Brown thread

Acrylic paints in brown, orange, yellow, turquoise, and olive

Clear cellophane tape

Bone folder

Small paintbrush

Pencil

Eraser

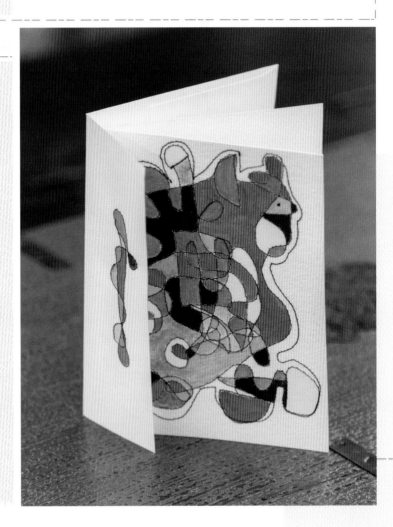

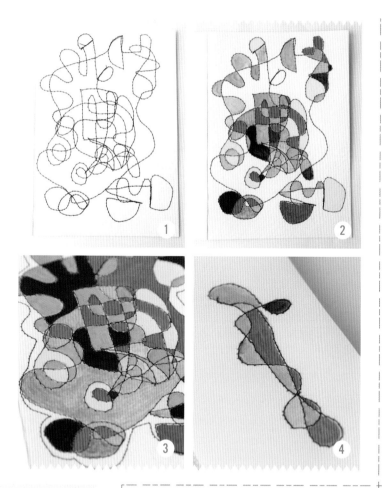

what you do

1 Fold the watercolor paper in half crosswise. Use the bone folder to make a clean crease.

2 With brown thread on the sewing machine and in the bobbin, free-motion stitch on just the right-hand portion of the card. Starting in the center, stitch in a random pattern, overlapping stitching and then working your way to the outer edges. Think about overlapping stitched lines in organic shapes with one continuous stitch line. **note:** *Stitch the center portion first and notice if there is a repeating pattern, then stitch the outer portions, repeating any patterns that you noticed.* FIG. 1

3 Paint the stitched sections of the card. Find portions on the card that have similar patterns and use just two colors to paint those sections. Look for images that might appear within the stitches. FIG. 2 In the card shown, I saw a little rabbit up in the top right portion, so I added a little brown dot for an eye.

4 Free-motion stitch around the perimeter of the painted stitched piece. FIG. 3

5 Adhere a strip of tape to the inside of the back flap of an envelope, centered and ½ inch (1.3 cm) from the flap edge. The tape helps to strengthen the envelope flap.

6 Free-motion stitch the envelope flap from the right side where the tape is. You may want to mark with a pencil, very lightly, where the tape is placed so that you can stitch right on top of the tape.

7 Trim the threads close to the stitching.

8 Paint the envelope flap. Erase any pencil marks. FIG. 4

note: *Here's an alternative way to mark stitch lines on the card. Follow step 1 as written above. Next, close your eyes and, using a pencil, mark the right side of the card in swirls and loops, again thinking of organic shapes as you mark the paper. Now, free-motion stitch on top of your pencil marks. When you are satisfied with the free-motion stitching, erase the pencil marks. Finish the card following steps 3-7.*

modern mug rug

Who says your cup of coffee doesn't need a stylish adornment.

what you need

Basic Sewing Kit (page 9)

Modern Mug Rug templates A–C (page 140)

Pieces or scraps of fabric in the following colors: tan with white dots, orange print, dark gray, gray with white dots, and light gray

⅛ yard (11.4 cm) of black print fabric for the binding

12 x 12 inch (30.5 x 30.5 cm) panel of white cotton batting

Black thread

Water-soluble fabric marker

Fabric glue stick

Temporary spray adhesive

Light box (optional)

what you do

note: *Use a ¼-inch (6-mm) seam allowance.*

1 Cut a panel from the tan-and-white-dot fabric that measures 2½ x 4 inches (6.4 x 10.2 cm).

2 Trace the three-flower template A onto a piece of paper and then, using a light box or window (page 13), transfer the flower drawing to the fabric with a water-soluble marker.

3 Using template B, cut out three flower centers from the orange print fabric and adhere the flower centers to the fabric with a glue stick.

4 Place the tan-and-white-dot panel (from step 1) on the cotton batting and cut out around the panel, leaving ¼ inch (6 mm) of batting all around.

5 With black thread on the sewing machine and black thread in the bobbin, free-motion stitch the flowers. Sew over the stitching again to achieve that sketchy look. FIG. 1

6 Cut a strip from the dark gray fabric that measures 7³⁄₈ x 2¼ inches (18.7 x 5.7 cm) and a piece that measures 2¾ x 3½ inches (7 x 8.9 cm).

7 Place these two panels on the cotton batting and cut around them, leaving ¼ inch (6 mm) of batting all around.

8 Using spray adhesive, adhere the batting pieces to the wrong side of the dark gray pieces.

9 From the gray dot fabric, cut out one rectangle that measures 1¼ x 1½ inches (3.2 x 3.8 cm).

10 Using the glue stick, center and adhere the rectangle on the smaller dark gray panel.

11 Free-motion stitch on the gray dot fabric and then several times around the gray dot fabric.

12 From the gray dot fabric, cut one rectangle that measures 1 x 1¼ inches (2.5 x 3.2 cm), one square that measures 1 x 1 inch (2.5 x 2.5 cm), and one more rectangle that measures 2 x 1 inches (5.1 x 2.5 cm).

13 Using the glue stick, adhere these three gray dot pieces to the long dark gray strip.

14 Free-motion stitch on the gray dot fabric and then several times around the gray dot fabric.

15 Cut the long dark gray strip to measure 7¼ x 2⅛ inches (18.4 x 5.4 cm). Cut the smaller dark gray panel down to measure 2⅝ x 3⅜ inches (6.7 x 8.6 cm).

16 Cut a piece of the light gray fabric that measures 5³⁄₈ x 3⁷⁄₈ inches (13.7 x 9.8 cm).

17 Place the light gray panel on the cotton batting and cut out around the panel, leaving ¼ inch (6 mm) of batting all around.

18 Using temporary spray adhesive, adhere the batting to the wrong side of the light gray piece.

19 Using template C, cut out three circles from the dark gray fabric. Using a glue stick, adhere the three pieces to the light gray panel.

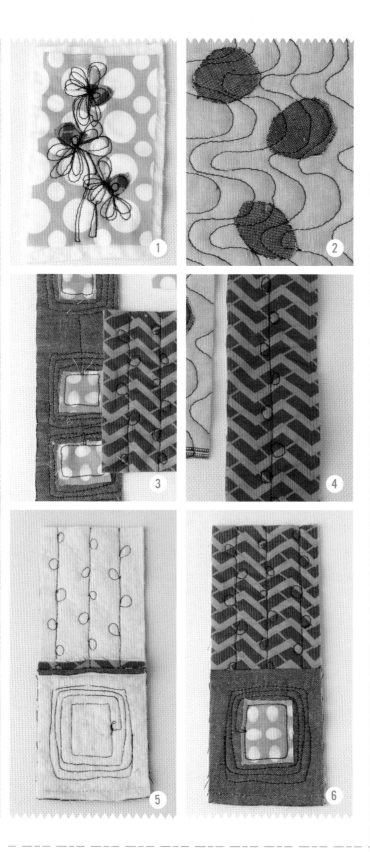

20 Free-motion stitch in a wavy pattern across the light gray panel, catching the dark gray circles as you stitch. Repeat several times to fill the entire fabric. FIG. 2

21 Trim the light gray panel to measure 5¼ x 3¾ inches (13.3 x 9.5 cm).

22 From the orange print fabric, cut 1 panel that measures 7¼ x 2¼ inches (18.4 x 5.7 cm) and another panel that measures 2⅞ x 4 inches (7.3 x 10.2 cm).

23 Place the orange panels on the cotton batting and cut out around each panel, leaving ¼ inch (6 mm) of batting all around.

24 Using spray adhesive, adhere the batting pieces to the wrong side of the orange panels.

25 Free-motion stitch the orange panels. Stitch in rows but every inch (2.5 cm) or so, create a little loop to one side of the row and then another little loop about an inch (2.5 cm) away on the opposite side. For the smaller orange panel, repeat this pattern of stitching three times total. For the larger panel, stitch in this manner one time down the center of the panel. FIGS. 3 & 4

26 Trim the threads close to the stitching.

27 Trim the larger orange panel to measure 7⅛ x 2 inches (18.1 x 5.1 cm) and the smaller panel to measure 2¾ x 3⅞ inches (7 x 9.8 cm).

28 With right sides facing, stitch the small orange panel from step 26 to the small dark gray panel. Press the seam allowance open. FIGS. 5 & 6

29 With right sides facing, stitch the tan dot panel to the light gray panel, along the 2¾-inch (7-cm) side. Press the seam allowance open. FIG. 7

30 With right sides facing, stitch the larger dark gray panel as shown in Figure 8. Press the seam allowance open.

31 With right sides facing, stitch the large orange panel to the bottom of the stitched panel from step 28. Press the seam allowance open.

32 With right side facing, stitch the panel from step 27 to the side of the main piece made in step 30. Press the seam allowance open. FIG. 9

33 For the back of the mug rug, cut a panel that measures 9½ x 6¾ inches (24.1 x 17.1 cm) from the orange print fabric.

10

11

12

34 Adhere this panel to the wrong side of the stitched panel, using spray adhesive.

35 Stitch around the panels, ⅛ inch (3 mm) from the seams, on just one side of the seam or to your liking.

36 From the black print fabric cut a strip that measure 2½ x 42 inches (6.4 x 106.7 cm). This strip will become the binding. Press the black strip in half lengthwise.

37 Bind the Mug Rug according to the binding instructions in the basics section on page 11. Fold the binding in at the corners to create mitered corners and hand-sew the binding in place. FIGS. 10–12

cutlery-stitched napkins

These napkins make a great housewarming gift.

what you need

Basic Sewing Kit (page 9)

Fork, Knife, and Spoon template
(page 140)

Set of 4 black cloth napkins,
each 19 x 19 inches
(48.3 x 48.3 cm)

White thread

what you do

1 Transfer the Fork, Knife, and Spoon template onto a napkin, 2½ inches (6.4 cm) up from the corner. **note:** *The easiest way to transfer the template is to use a light color wax-free carbon paper (page 13).*

2 With white thread on the sewing machine and in the bobbin, free-motion stitch the traced template. Stitch back over the first stitching to get a sketchy look.

3 Trim the threads close to the stitching.

4 Lightly press the napkin.

5 Repeat steps 1–4 for the remaining three napkins.

strip-pieced place mats

Place mats are the perfect finishing touch to any tablescape.

what you need

Basic Sewing Kit (page 9)

⅓ yard (30.5 cm) of navy blue cotton fabric

Scraps of various green and blue solids and print cotton fabrics

½ yard (45.7 cm) of light blue cotton for backing

¼ yard (22.9 cm) of navy blue print cotton fabric for the binding

½ yard (45.7 cm) of cotton batting

Thread in tan and white

Temporary spray adhesive

what you do

note: *Use a ¼-inch (6-mm) seam allowance.*

1 Cut strips that measure the following sizes. **note:** *The strips are numbered from 1 through 7, moving from left to right. The fabric pieces are cut in order, from top to bottom.* FIG. 1

Strip 1: Navy, 3½ x 5 inches (8.9 x 12.7 cm); green, 3½ x 4 inches (8.9 x 10.2 cm); navy, 3½ x 5½ inches (8.9 x 14 cm)

Strip 2: Navy, 2½ x 3½ inches (6.4 x 8.9 cm); green, 2½ x 7 inches (6.4 x 17.8 cm); navy, 2½ x 4 inches (6.4 x 10.2 cm)

Strip 3: Navy, 4½ x 4½ inches (14 x 11.4 cm); cut 2 green, 2½ x 5½ inches (6.4 x 14 cm) each; navy, 4½ x 4½ inches (14 x 11.4 cm)

Strip 4: Navy, 3 x 3½ inches (7.6 x 8.9 cm); green, 3 x 8½ inches (7.6 x 21.6 cm); navy, 3 x 2½ inches (7.6 x 6.4 cm)

Strip 5: Green, 2 x 6 inches (5.1 x 15.2 cm); navy, 2 x 3 inches (5.1 x 7.6 cm); green, 2 x 5½ inches (5.1 x 14 cm)

Strip 6: Navy, 3 x 4½ inches (7.6 x 11.4 cm); green, 3 x 6 inches (7.6 x 15.2 cm); navy 3 x 4 inches (7.6 x 10.2 cm)

Strip 7: Navy, 2 x 5 inches (5.1 x 12.7 cm); green, 2 x 4¾ inches (5.1 x 12 cm); navy 2 x 4¾ inches (5.1 x 12 cm)

2 With tan thread on the sewing machine and in the bobbin and starting with strip 1, stitch the fabric pieces together with right sides facing and aligning the short ends. Stitch them together in the order that they were cut. FIG. 2

3 Repeat step 2 for all other strips except strip 3.

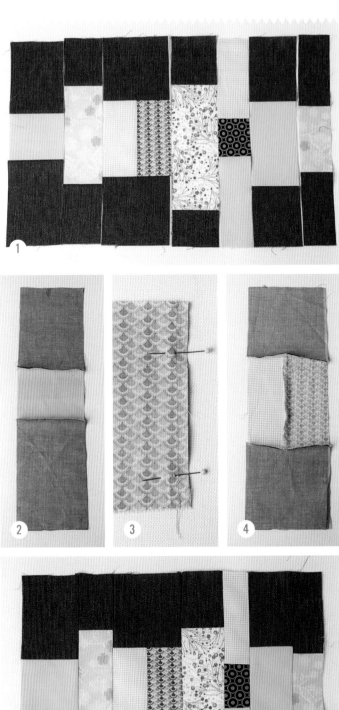

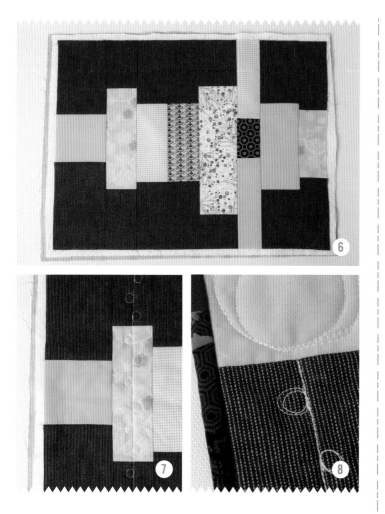

8 Place the light blue backing panel on the work surface, right side down. Place the batting on top of the backing and then place the pieced top onto the batting, right side up.

9 Use temporary spray adhesive to lightly adhere the pieces together: Gently lift up a small portion of the batting and lightly spray the wrong side of the backing. Gently lift up a small portion of the pieced place mat top and lightly spray the batting. Pat down the layers to make sure that the spray adhesive has all the layers adhered together. FIG. 6

10 With white thread on the sewing machine and in the bobbin free-motion stitch vertically through all the layers. Start stitching at the center top of strip 4. Sew straight down, stitching a small "bubble" every inch (2.5 cm) or so.

11 Repeat step 10 for all the other strips, working from the center of the place mat (roughly strip 4) to the outer strips. For a couple of the strips, free-motion stitch larger bubbles on the green fabric. FIGS. 7 & 8

12 Stitch back over all the stitching one more time to give the place mat a sketchy look.

13 Cut a strip of binding fabric that measures 2¼ x 70 inches (5.7 x 177.8 cm). Follow the binding instructions on page 11 in the basics section to finish the place mat. **note:** *You will have to cut a couple of shorter strips and then stitch them together to make a strip that measures 70 inches.*

14 Flip the place mat over and check out the stitching on the back!

4 Stitch strip 3 as follows: Sew the green pieces together, long sides aligned, right sides facing. Press the seam allowance to one side. Now stitch the navy pieces to this green pieced panel, right sides facing and short ends aligned. FIGS 3 & 4

5 Press the seam allowances toward the navy pieces. Stitch the strips together with right sides facing and aligning the long sides. FIG. 5

6 Press all the seam allowances to one side.

7 Cut out panels from the batting and the light blue fabric that measure 18½ x 14½ inches (47 x 36.8 cm) each.

pet portrait pillow

Snuggle up with a good book and your furry friend!

what you need

Basic Sewing Kit (page 9)

Photo of your dog, cat, horse, hamster, or other pet or templates A–J if you are making the pillow with this pup on it (page 141)

¼ yard (22.9 cm) of fusible web

¼ yard (22.9 cm) of teal print fabric

Scraps of fabric in lime green, white print, blue print, and black

½ yard (45.7 cm) of osnaburg or tan linen fabric

Thread in black and off-white

Pillow form, 16 x 12 inches (40.6 x 30.5 cm)

Acrylic paints in white and black

Water-soluble fabric marker

Paintbrush

2 sheets of copy paper

Chopstick or wooden knitting needle

what you do

note: *Use a ¼-inch (6-mm) seam allowance.*

1 Scan your photo and upload the image into photo-editing software. Create a black-and-white image; increase the contrast so the light and dark areas of the photo are very prominent. Enlarge the image to be 9 inches (22.9 cm) high. Print out two copies of the image. If you are making the pillow with my pup on it, trace template A onto the pieces of paper.

2 Cut out one copy, flip it over, and trace it onto the paper side of the fusible web. note: *If you are making the pillow with my pup on it, you do not need to flip any of the templates over; I have done that for you already.* FIG. 1

3 Following the manufacturer's directions, fuse the web to the back of the teal print fabric. Once cooled, cut out the shape on the traced line. FIGS. 2 & 3

4 With the second copy of the photo, cut out around the high-contrast areas. For example I cut out around the muzzle and forehead, the lower jaw and neck, inside the ears, chin, nose, eyeballs, and three feet. If you are making the pillow with my pup on it, then trace and cut out templates B–J.

5 Flip your pieces over and trace them on the paper side of the fusible web. note: *Again, if you are making the pillow with my pup on it, you do not need to flip any of the templates over; I have done that for you already.* FIG. 4

6 Following the manufacturer's directions, fuse the web to the wrong

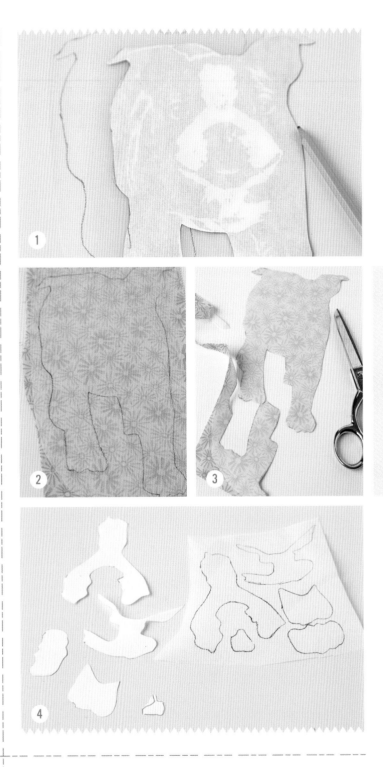

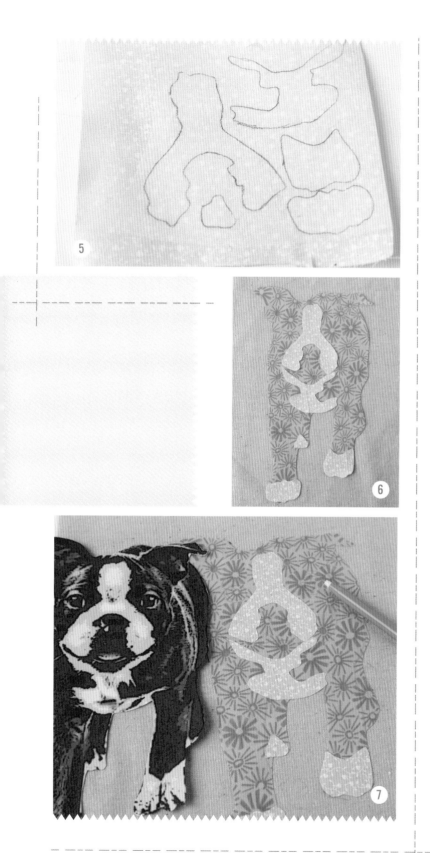

5

6

7

side of the lime green fabric, white print fabric, blue fabric, and black fabric. Once cooled, cut out the shapes. FIG. 5

7 Cut a panel of osnaburg that measures 12 x 13 inches (30.5 x 33 cm).

8 Peel the paper backing off of the teal fused shape and place it on the osnaburg panel, 3 inches (7.6 cm) from the left side and 2 inches (5.1 cm) up from the bottom.

9 Following the manufacturer's directions, fuse the teal piece to the osnaburg.

10 Peel the paper backing off the lime green shapes and place them on the teal shape. Refer to your black-and-white image to get the placement correct. FIG. 6

11 Following the manufacturer's directions, fuse the pieces to the teal piece. FIG. 7

12 Peel the paper backing off the white fused pieces and place them on the teal fabric. Again, refer to the black-and-white image to find the correct placement.

13 Following the manufacturer's directions, fuse the pieces to the teal piece.

14 Peel the paper backing off of the black fabric pieces and place them on the teal fabric. Again, refer to the black-and-white image to find the correct placement.

15 Using the water-soluble marker, draw detail around the eyes and mouth.

16 With black thread on the sewing machine and in the bobbin, free-motion stitch around the fused pieces. Stitch a second time around the pieces to give the piece a sketchy look.

17 Free-motion stitch the eyes and the mouth a couple of times. Refer to the black-and-white image to see if there is any other detail that could be stitched at this time to give the image a bit of character. Trim the threads close to the stitching.

18 Dab the drawn areas with a damp cloth and then lightly press the stitched panel.

19 Paint in highlights around the eyes and nose with white paint. FIG. 8

20 From the white print fabric cut a strip that measures 1¼ x 13 inches (3.2 x 33 cm).

21 Change the sewing machine to have white thread on the top and in the bobbin.

22 With right sides facing, pin then stitch the white strip to the stitched panel along the panel's left-hand side. FIG. 9

23 From the lime green, blue, teal, and white scraps, cut ten rectangles that measure 2¾ x 3 inches (7 x 7.6 cm) each.

24 Stitch together five pieces, right sides facing, along the short sides. Press the seam allowances up.

25 Stitch the remaining five pieces together, right sides facing, along the short sides. Press the seam allowances down.

26 Stitch these two strips together along the long edge, matching seams. Press the seam allowance to one side. FIG. 10

27 With right sides facing, pin these patchwork pieces to the left side of the pillow front, along the white strip. Stitch in place and lightly press the seam allowance toward the white strip.

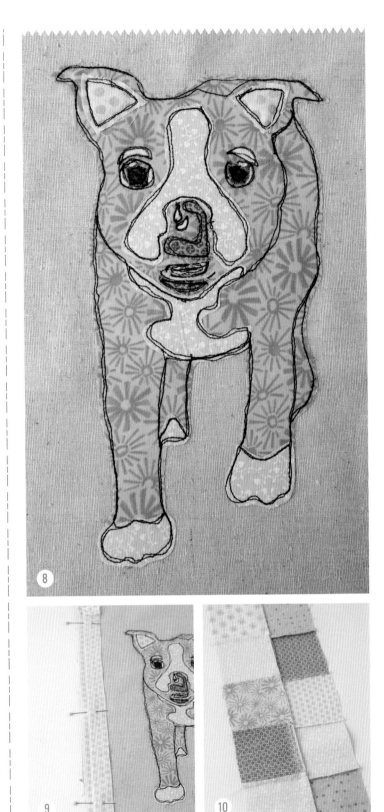

8

9

10

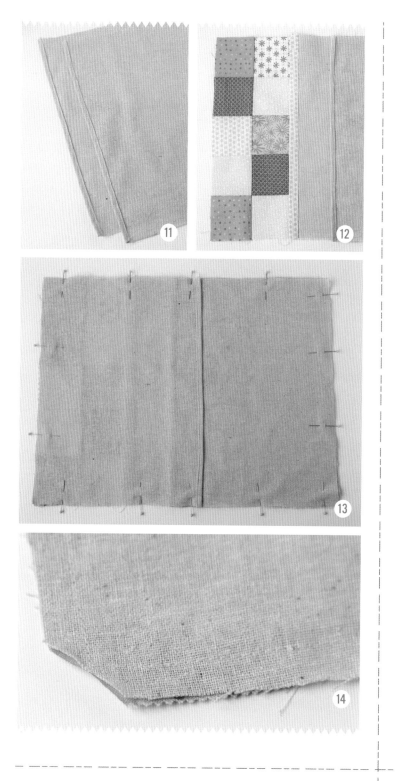

28 For the pillow back, cut two panels from the osnaburg that measure 10 x 13 inches (25.4 x 33 cm) each.

29 Press under one long edge of one of the pillow back pieces by ¼ inch (6 mm). Press this same edge under another ¼ inch (6 mm). Stitch the hem in place close to the fold. Repeat for the other pillow back piece. FIG. 11

30 Lay the pillow front on a flat surface, right side facing up. Pin one of the backs to the pillow front, right sides facing and aligned with the right-hand side of the pillow front. Pin in place. FIG. 12

31 Pin the other back piece to the left-hand side of the pillow front, again right sides facing and aligned with the left side. **note:** *These two back pieces will overlap at the center.* FIG. 13

32 Stitch around the perimeter of the pillow, pivoting at the corners.

33 Trim the corners at a diagonal and turn the pillow right side out. FIG. 14 Poke the corners out with a chopstick, and then lightly press the pillow.

34 Insert the pillow form into the pillow cover.

road-trippin' hoop art

Hoop art is a great addition to any gallery wall.

what you need

Basic Sewing Kit (page 9)

Road-trippin' hoop art templates (page 142)

Natural color linen, 11 x 11 inches (27.9 x 27.9 cm)

White cotton fabric, 11 x 11 inches (27.9 x 27.9 cm)

Fabric scraps in white, orange print, light blue print, peach print, black and aqua

9 x 4 inch (22.8 x 10.2 cm) panel of aqua color linen

Thread in black and white

10 inches (25.4 cm) of black ribbon

10 x 10 inch (25.4 x 25.4 cm) square of fusible web

Water-soluble fabric marker

Wood embroidery hoop, 7 inches (17.8 cm) in diameter

Temporary spray adhesive

what you do

1 Place the linen square on top of the white cotton square.

2 Place the embroidery hoop onto the linen and trace around the outer edge with a water-soluble fabric marker. FIG. 1

3 Trace the van and suitcases template on to a piece of paper.

4 Place a panel of fusible web onto the van with the paper side up. Trace around the entire body of the van. FIG. 2

5 With a smaller panel of fusible web, trace around the lower portion of the van. With another small panel of fusible web, trace around the tires and then trace around the luggage, leaving a little space in between the pieces of luggage. FIG. 3

6 Following the manufacturer's instructions, fuse the van to the wrong side of the white fabric, fuse the lower portion of the van to the wrong side of the orange print fabric, fuse the tires to the wrong side of the black fabric, and fuse the suitcases to the wrong side of the light blue, peach, and aqua fabrics.

7 Cut out around these fused shapes and then peel off the paper backing.

8 Center the white van on the linen 2 inches (5.1 cm) from the bottom marked edge. Following the manufacturer's instructions, fuse it in place.

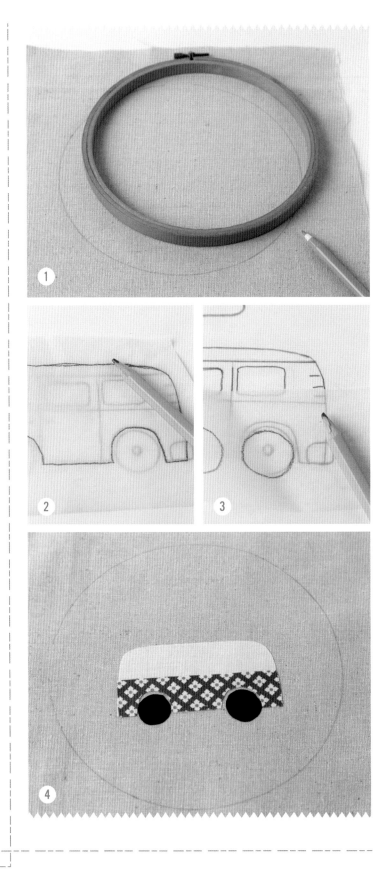

9 Fuse the lower portion of the van on top of the lower portion of the white van. Fuse the tires in place. FIG. 4

10 Referring to the traced van, use a water-soluble fabric marker and draw in the windows, doors, and bumpers on the van. FIG. 5

11 With black thread on the machine and in the bobbin, free-motion stitch around the fused shapes. Stitch back over the original stitching to give the piece a sketchy look. Stitch in a few details such as the steering wheel, bumpers, and the headlights. FIG. 6

12 Following the manufacturer's instructions, fuse the luggage to the top of the van.

13 With black thread on the machine and in the bobbin, free-motion stitch around the luggage, the luggage handles and latches. FIG. 7

14 With white thread on the machine and the bobbin, free-motion stitch around the tires.

15 Using a water-soluble fabric marker, draw in a road on the natural-color linen. Make sure that the road is narrower at the right and wider on the left.

16 With black thread on the sewing machine and in the bobbin, free-motion stitch the road. FIG. 8

17 Trim the threads close to the stitching.

18 Place the aqua linen in the lower portion under the road and then trim the linen so that it follows the outer curve of the line drawn in step 2. Use temporary spray adhesive to adhere the piece. FIG. 9

19 With white thread on the machine and the bobbin, free-motion stitch the aqua piece in place. FIG. 10

20 Attach the wood embroidery hoop. FIG. 11

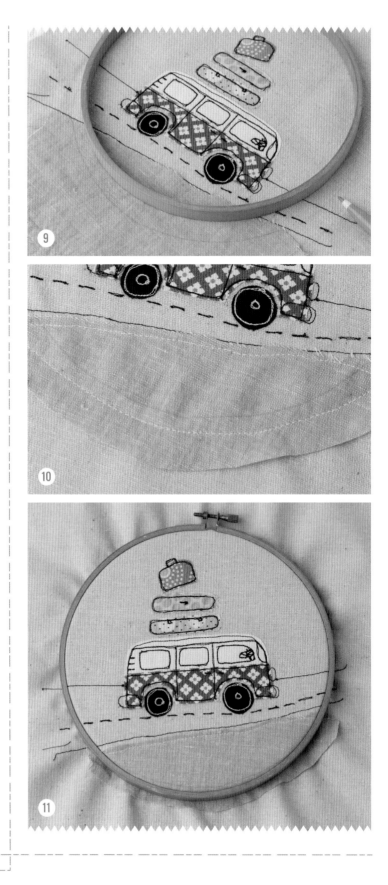

21 Mark 1 inch (2.5 cm) from the edge of the hoop and cut out around the hoop along this marking. FIG. 12

22 Thread the hand-sewing needle with a double strand of white thread and sew a long basting stitch around the hoop, ¼ inch (6 mm) from the cut edge. Gather up the fabric to the back side as you stitch and then knot the thread when you reach the beginning. FIG. 13

23 Attach the black ribbon to the top of the hoop. FIG. 14

gift tags

These tags can be given as gifts or used to adorn packages of your choosing.

what you need

Basic Sewing Kit (page 9)

Gift Tags templates A–E
(page 142)

Scraps of fabric in lime green,
deep red, gray, orange, and
turquoise

Black thread

Glue stick

Shipping tag, 2⅜ x 4¾ inches
(6 x 12 cm)

Acrylic paints in silver, black,
and white

Piece of book text, 1½ x ¾ inches
(3.8 x 1.9 cm)

Black fine-tip permanent marker

10 inches (25.4 cm) of ½-inch
(1.3 cm) wide black rayon ribbon

Small paintbrush

what you do

1 Trace templates A–E onto pieces of paper and cut out the shapes.

2 Pin template A onto the lime green fabric and cut around the shape.

3 Pin template B onto the deep red fabric and cut out around the shape.

4 Pin template C onto the gray fabric and cut out around the shape.

5 Pin template D onto the orange fabric and cut out around the shape.

6 Pin template E onto the turquoise fabric and cut out around the shape.

7 Using the glue stick, adhere the lime green circle to the top right-hand portion of the tag. FIG. 1 With black thread on the sewing machine and in the bobbin, free-motion stitch zigzag lines across the center and then add little petals or scallops around the outer edge. Finally, stitch a "stem" straight down to the bottom edge. FIG. 2

8 Using the glue stick, adhere the deep red piece to the tag, on the left-hand side and overlapping the lime green flower. Add the gray piece to the center of the deep red piece. FIG. 3

9 Free-motion stitch the red piece in place, following the curve several times, placing the lines ¼ inch (6 mm) apart. Free-motion stitch the gray piece in place, again, following the curve several times, ⅛ inch (3 mm) apart. Free-motion stitch a stem from the red piece down to the bottom edge.

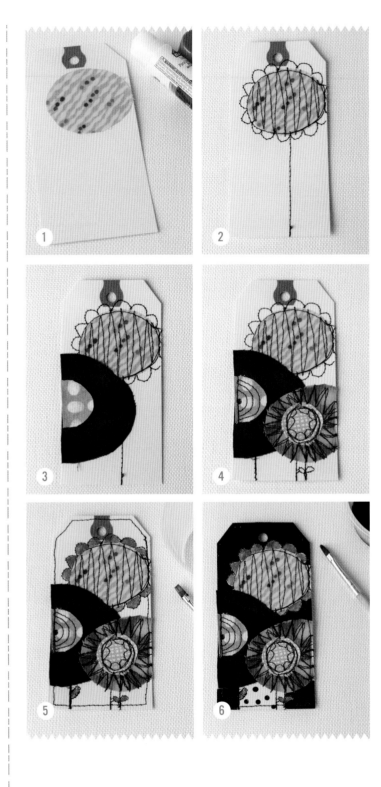

10 Using the glue stick, adhere the orange piece to the tag, overlapping the deep red piece. Adhere the turquoise circle to the center of the orange piece.

11 Free-motion stitch zigzag lines around the orange piece, radiating out from the center. Free-motion stitch around the turquoise circle and then stitch little scallops inside the center.

12 Free-motion stitch little leaves on the stems. FIG. 4

13 Trim the threads close to the stitching.

14 With silver paint, fill in the flower petals on the top right flower and the leaves on the stems. FIG. 5

15 With black paint, fill in the rest of the exposed tag, avoiding the small portion between the stems.

16 Dip the rounded end of the paintbrush into the paint and add dots between the stems. FIGS. 6 & 7

17 Paint a thin coat of white paint on the panel of book text. Set aside to dry. FIG. 8

18 Paint a thin coat of white paint to the front of the painted book text. Set aside to dry. Paint a thin coat to the back side and set aside to dry.

19 With the permanent marker, hand-letter the word "Thanks" on the book-text piece. **note:** *Individualize or personalize this with almost any word or greeting that fits.* FIG. 9

20 Free-motion stitch the book text to the tag. FIG. 10

21 Attach the black ribbon. FIG. 11

beach cruiser pouch

The perfect pouch to store all your necessities.
You can even put in your Market Tote!

what you need

Basic Sewing Kit (page 9)

Beach Cruiser Pouch Templates A and B (page 142)

Piece of white polka-dot fabric, 7½ x 5½ inches (19 x 14 cm)

Variety of coordinating fabrics such as orange/gold print for the zipper pull, and gold, orange and teal prints.

Piece of fabric for the back of the pouch, 15 x 10 inches (38.1 x 25.4 cm)

Piece of fabric for the lining, 32 x 10 inches (81.3 x 25.4 cm)

Piece of water-soluble stabilizer (such as Sulky Solvy), 7½ x 5½ inches (19 x 14 cm)

Lightweight cotton batting

Thread in red and teal

9-inch (22.9 cm) red zipper

Sheet of paper, 11 x 14 inches (27.9 x 35.6 cm)

Black fine-tip permanent marker

Zipper foot

what you do

note: *Use a ¼-inch (6-mm) seam allowance.*

1 Center and trace template A on the piece of water-soluble stabilizer.

2 Pin the stabilizer panel onto the white fabric and then stitch around the perimeter with a basting stitch. FIG. 1

3 With red thread on the sewing machine and in the bobbin, free-motion stitch the bicycle. Stitch the bicycle again to give it a sketchy look. Trim the threads close to the stitching. FIG. 2

4 Tear away the stabilizer around the bicycle and then, following the manufacturer's directions, dissolve any remaining stabilizer in warm water and remove the basting stitch. Set the panel aside to dry. Once dry, lightly press the panel. FIG. 3

5 Trim the white stitched panel to measure 7 x 5 inches (17.8 x 12.7 cm).

6 Cut one of the print scraps to measure 4½ x 5 inches (11.4 x 12.7 cm). Stitch this panel to the left-hand side of the bicycle panel, right sides facing.

7 Cut another print fabric scrap to measure 3 x 5 inches (7.6 x 12.7 cm) and then stitch this panel to the right-hand side of the bicycle, right sides facing. Press both seam allowances toward the print fabrics. FIG. 4

8 Cut a print scrap to measure 14½ x 3½ inches (36.8 x 8.9 cm) and stitch this panel to the bottom of the bicycle panel, right sides facing. Press the seam allowance toward the print fabric.

9 Cut a print fabric scrap to measure 12 x 2½ inches (30.5 x 6.4 cm) and stitch this panel to the top of the bicycle panel, centered and with right sides facing. Press the seam allowance toward the print fabric. FIG. 5

10 Cut a small print scrap to measure 4½ x 1¼ inches (11.4 x 3.2 cm). Press all the edges under ¼ inch (6 mm) and then pin this panel to the bottom of the bicycle panel, under the stitched bicycle. FIG. 6 Stitch this panel, with white thread, in place close to the folded edges.

11 Trace template B onto the paper, place the template on the stitched panel, and cut out the pouch front. Double-check to make sure that the bicycle panel is parallel to the bottom of the pouch template. FIG. 7

12 Cut one template B from the backing fabric.

13 Place the stitched front piece onto the batting and cut the batting ¼ inch (6 mm) away from the cut edge of the front piece. FIG. 8

14 Place the back piece on the batting and cut out the batting right at the cut edge of the back piece.

15 Pin and then stitch the batting pieces to the pouch front, close to the cut of the front piece. Repeat for the back piece.

16 With teal thread on the sewing machine and in the bobbin, free-motion stitch scallops onto the outer fabric panels. Free-motion stitch a stem and loops onto the white panel and then continue up and onto the printed panel. Stop and start the stitching so that the stem appears to be growing behind the bicycle. FIG. 9

17 Place a mark on the right side at the end of the zipper 7½ inches (19 cm) from the zipper stop.

18 Cut two pieces of fabric that measure 1¼ x 1¼ inches (3.2 x 3.2 cm) each.

19 Fold one short end of one of the pieces cut in step 18 under ¼ inch (6 mm) and then stitch this edge to the end of the zipper near the zipper stop. Repeat for the other fabric piece and then stitch this piece to the other end of the zipper at the mark that was made in step 17.
note: *The zipper will extend beyond the fabric on the end where the zipper stops when open; trim the zipper down to match the fabric there.* FIG. 10

20 Pin the zipper to the top edge of the front pouch, right sides facing. Line up the edge of the zipper with the top edge of the pouch front. Using a zipper foot, stitch the zipper in place using ¼-inch (6-mm) seam allowance. FIG. 11

21 Pin the zipper to the top edge of the back pouch, right sides facing. Line up the edge of the zipper with the top edge of the pouch back. Using a zipper foot, stitch the zipper in place using ¼-inch (6-mm) seam allowance. FIG. 12

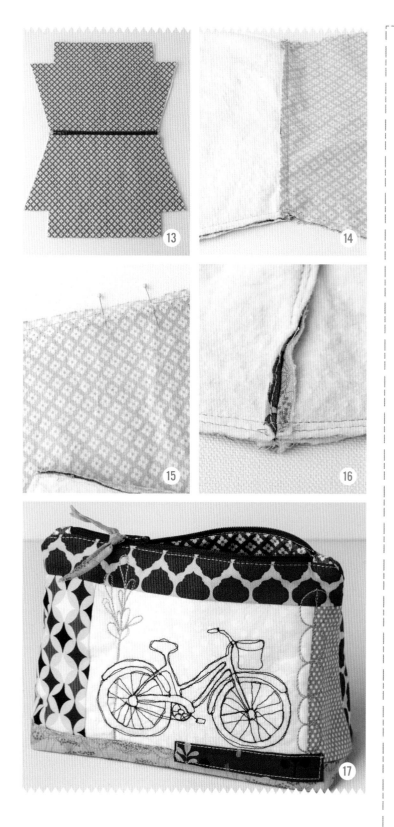

22 Pin one of the lining pieces to the zipper, right side of the lining fabric to the wrong side of the zipper. Repeat for the other lining piece. FIG. 13

23 Lay the pouch flat so that the two outer pouch pieces are facing each other and the two lining pieces are facing each other. FIG. 14

24 Pin and then stitch the bottom portion of the outer pouch.

25 Pin the bottom portion of the lining together. Stitch the bottom of the lining, leaving a 4-inch (10.2-cm) gap in the center. This gap will allow you to turn the pouch right side out. FIG. 15

26 Pin and then stitch the side seams.

27 Fold the corner out with right sides facing and then stitch across the corner, making sure that the seam allowance is opened up. Repeat for the other side and then for both corners in the lining. FIG. 16

28 Turn the pouch right side out through the gap in the lining.

29 Turn the seam allowance in at the gap and stitch the gap closed. Push the lining to the inside of the pouch.

30 Cut a strip of orange print fabric that measures 1½ x 6 inches (3.8 x 15.2 cm). Press the strip in half lengthwise and then press the outer edges in toward the centerfold. Stitch close to the folded edges.

31 Tie the strip to the zipper pull. FIG. 17

templates

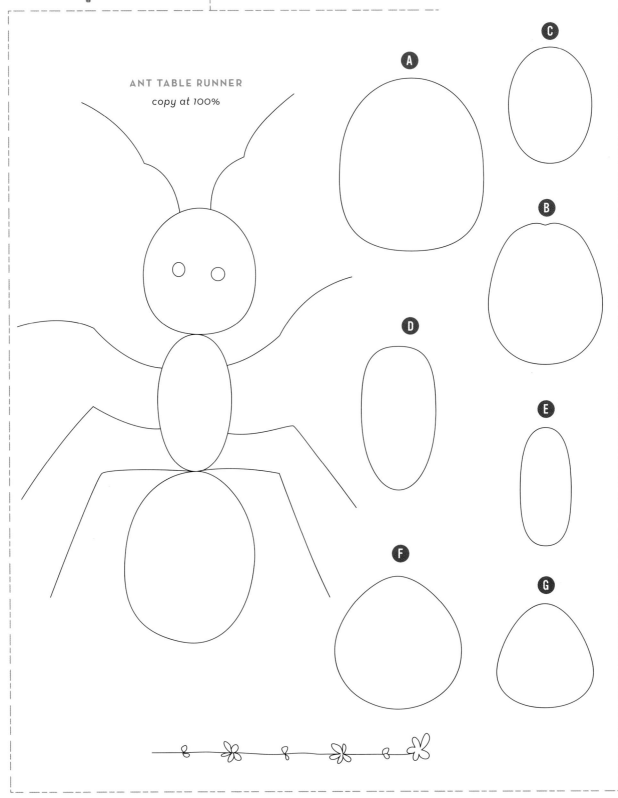

ANT TABLE RUNNER

copy at 100%

A

C

B

D

E

F

G

FRENCH PRESS APRON
copy at 100%

A

OWL AND FEATHER
BOOKMARK
copy at 100%

OWL AND FEATHER BOOKMARK

copy at 100%

FABRIC COLLAGE BULLETIN BOARD

enlarge 200%

FABRIC COLLAGE
BULLETIN BOARD
enlarge 250%

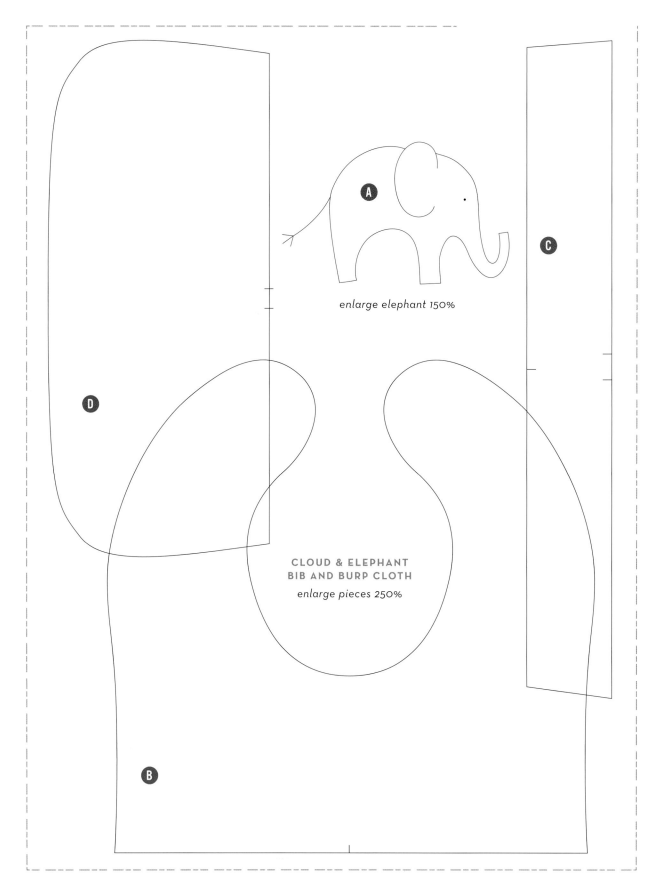

enlarge elephant 150%

CLOUD & ELEPHANT
BIB AND BURP CLOTH

enlarge pieces 250%

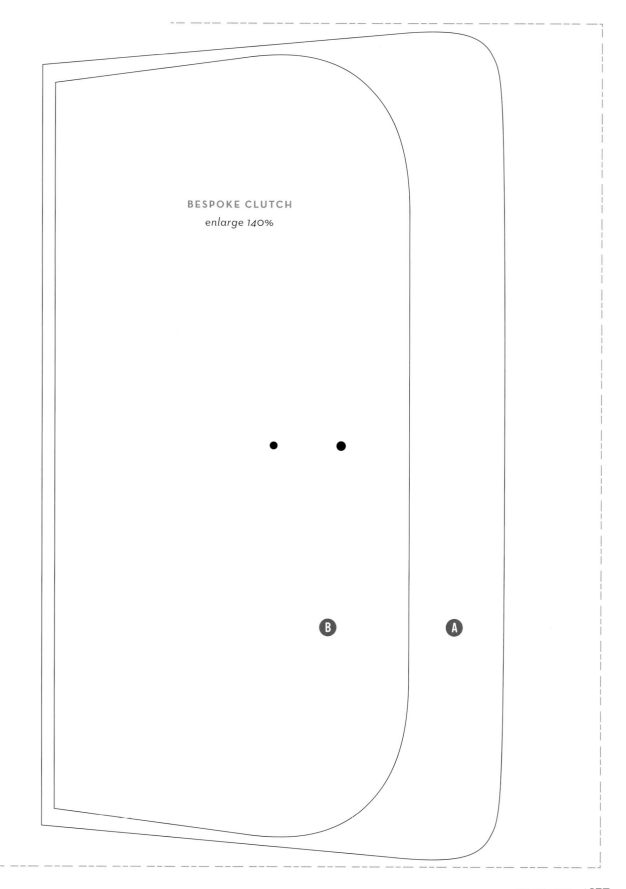

BESPOKE CLUTCH
enlarge 140%

B A

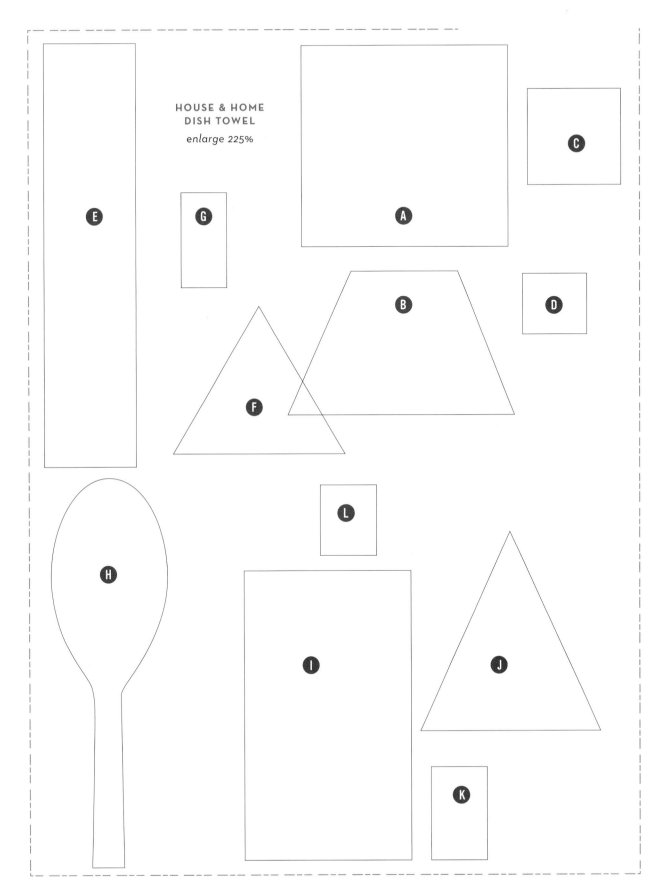

HOUSE & HOME
DISH TOWEL
enlarge 225%

FELT ORNAMENTS
copy at 100%

FLORAL-PAINTED TABLET COVER
enlarge 150%

A

WHEAT & HONEY
MARKET TOTE
enlarge 150%

B

MODERN MUG RUG
enlarge 125%

B

C

FORK

KNIFE

SPOON

CUTLERY-STITCHED NAPKINS
enlarge 175%

A

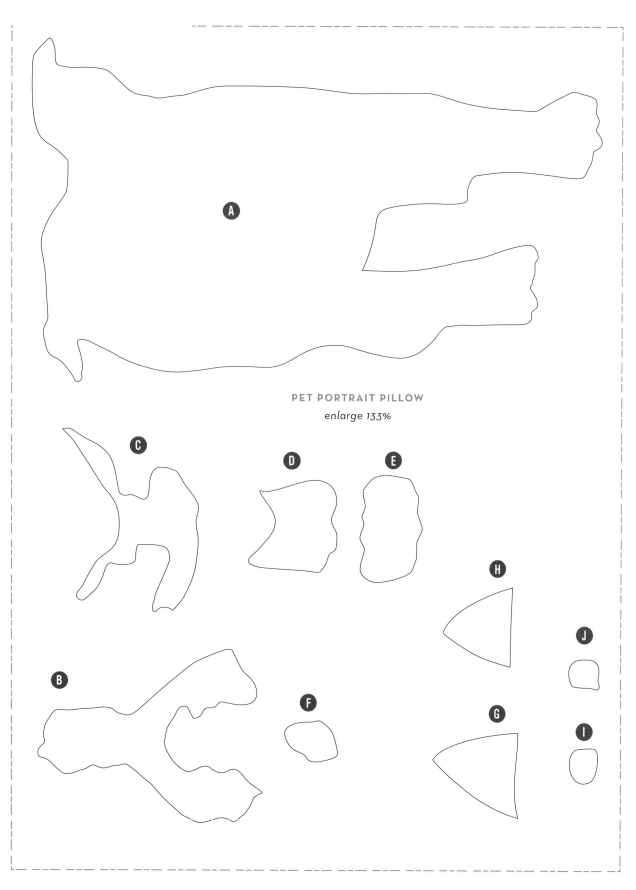

PET PORTRAIT PILLOW
enlarge 133%

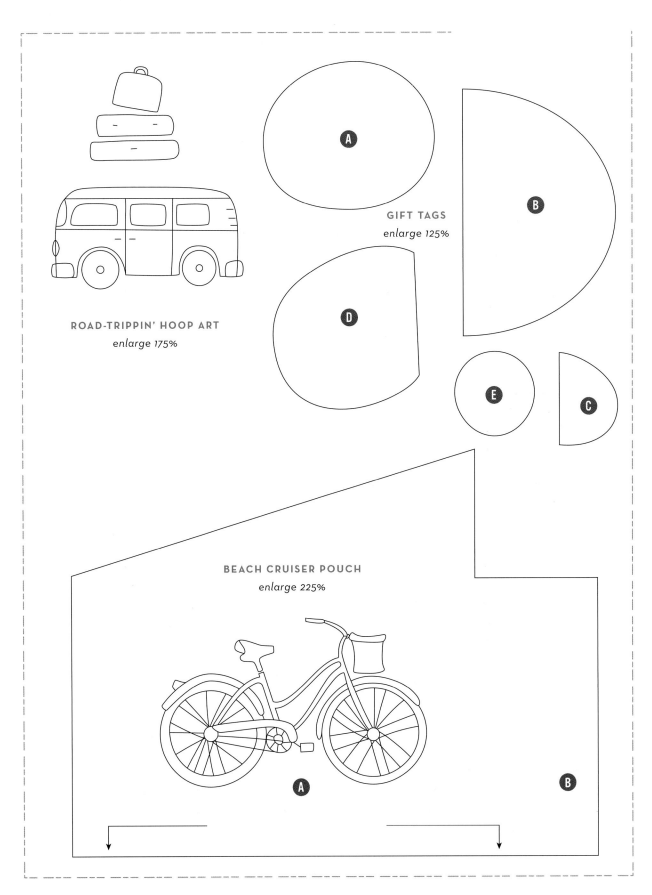

ROAD-TRIPPIN' HOOP ART
enlarge 175%

GIFT TAGS
enlarge 125%

A

B

D

E

C

BEACH CRUISER POUCH
enlarge 225%

A

B

ABOUT THE AUTHOR

CYNTHIA SHAFFER is a mixed-media artist, creative sewer, and photographer whose love of sewing can be traced back to childhood. At the age of six, she learned to sew and in no time was designing and sewing clothing for herself and others. After earning a degree in textiles from California State University, Long Beach, Cynthia worked for ten years as the owner of a company that specialized in the design and manufacture of sportswear. Numerous books and magazines have featured Cynthia's art and photography work: she is the author of *Stash Happy Patchwork* (Lark, 2011), *Stash Happy Appliqué* (Lark, 2012), coauthor of *Serge It* (Lark, 2014), and author of *Coastal Crafts* (Lark, 2015). In her spare time Cynthia knits, crochets, paints, and dabbles in all sorts of crafts. If she's not crafting, Cynthia can be found at the gym lifting weights, kickboxing, or in the back bay of Newport Beach with her paddling friends. Cynthia lives with her family and pets in Southern California. For more information, visit Cynthia online at cynthiashaffer.typepad.com or www.cynthiashaffer.com.

ABOUT THE CONTRIBUTING DESIGNER

JEN OSBORN (designer of the Little Cloth Buckets and Wheat & Honey Market Tote) is a third generation maker who lives in the heart of rural Michigan. In 2003 she developed an innovative mixed media technique using fire to manipulate transparency images, and has been featured in a dozen books. She's spent time among magazine pages as both a published artist and as a columnist while teaching her techniques online and across the US; her first solo book *Mixed and Stitched: Fabric Inspiration and How-To's for the Mixed Media Artist* was published in 2011. Visit Jen online at www.themessynest.com, instagram & twitter: themessynest.

ACKNOWLEDGMENTS

This book would not have made it to the printing press and into your hands if it were not for my editor, Diana Ventimiglia. Yes, she was calm, cool, and collected when I was harried, hot, and frazzled, and for that I am forever grateful! I'd also like to acknowledge and thank the entire team of artists and experts at Sterling Publishing / Lark Crafts that pulled out all the stops to crank through this book to make it happen in warp speed.

Thank you to all my friends who let me invade their homes and spaces to photograph all the stitched gifts. I'd like to thank artist and friend Becky Porcella for sharing her ant illustrations with me and for allowing me to use them in the Ant Runner!

To my parents: They believed in my gift of creativity and never questioned my passion for sewing and creating. Thank you, Mom and Dad, for instilling in me the value of finishing what you start. Thanks also to my kids, Corry and Cameron, who's opinions and critiques I value to the moon and back. And a special thank you to my husband, Scott, who allowed my stitched crafts to spill out of my studio and into the various rooms in our house. And, of course, much love to my Boston terriers, Harper and Berklee, who kept me company all day long while I sewed, crafted, and created *Stitched Gifts*!

INDEX

note: *Page numbers in italics indicate projects (and templates).*